Praise for
LEADERSHIP, EXCELLENCE, AND A ROYAL COACHMAN

"This is a book bursting with profound wisdom gained from real-life experiences. It is a book to be retained as a valuable reference to anyone in a leadership position. I highly recommend it!"

HERB OBERG

Sergeant USMC retired; Captain, Snohomish County Sheriff's Office, Washington, retired

"I am really impressed with the insightful pearls of wisdom that are packed into 131 pages. It really reads well. I think this book will appeal to people of varied occupations, gender, and interests."

DAVID SMITH

Principal, Whitwell Elementary School, Whitwell, Tennessee

"This is a great book, very to the point and easy to read, which I believe is the key to a book that appeals to a wide group."

PETER FOY

Chief Executive Officer, PCF Insurance Services, Woodland Hills, CA

"This book is a must-read for all leaders who desire to see their business or organization grow and succeed. This is not your basic ho-hum leadership book. Gausman's unique and transparent approach to leadership is woven between personal examples from fly fishing and numerous personal vocational experiences. His unique observations and clearly spelled out tried and true leadership principles will encourage you to step it up to become a better leader. As a leader who works cross-culturally in leadership training, I was personally challenged by the book and am looking forward to sharing these valuable leadership insights, possibly with a fishing rod and coachman fly in hand."

RODNEY HUSON
President, Equipping to Serve Brazil Ministries,
Brazil, South America

Leadership, Excellence, and a Royal Coachman:
Observations from a Lifetime of Transitions from
Corporate Life to Fly Fishing Guide

by Ryan Gausman

ISBN 978-1-63393-967-7

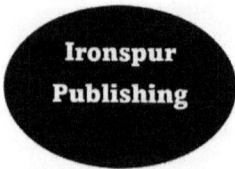

Published by

**Ironspur
Publishing**

Rogausman@gmail.com

RYAN GAUSMAN

LEADERSHIP,
EXCELLENCE,
— AND —
A ROYAL
COACHMAN

OBSERVATIONS FROM A LIFETIME OF TRANSITIONS FROM CORPORATE LIFE TO FLY FISHING GUIDE

Ironspur
Publishing

TABLE OF CONTENTS

INTRODUCTION

MANY WORDS ARE USED to define excellence. They include "very good," "outstanding," and "of the highest and finest quality." The Bible talks about excellence in Daniel 6:3: "Then this Daniel became distinguished above all the other high officials and satraps because an excellent spirit was in him." Clearly then, excellence in life and in his way of living was unusual to the extent that an excellent spirit distinguished Daniel above all of his peers.

In the early 1980s, authors Thomas J. Peters and Robert H. Waterman Jr. wrote the book *In Search of Excellence: Lessons from America's Best-Run Companies* in which they detailed the results of their research into what made certain companies great. The title of the book was their answer: They all searched for excellence every day. The companies that did so were unusual and stood out from all of their peers. This showed not only on their bottom line but in their reputation around the community where they operated. In other words, everybody who was associated with them—employees, customers, and competitors—recognized and appreciated that they were excellent.

I worked in a leadership role for one of the retail companies, Nordstrom, that Peters and Waterman featured in their book. At Nordstrom, I experienced the things they identified. I was in a position to work directly with and spend a considerable amount of one-on-one time with the corporate leadership. They not only demanded the very best from every associate of their company, they also put in place a corporate culture that required, empowered, and enabled people to be their best. Those of us in leadership positions were tasked with identifying and grooming the future leaders of the company. It was a time of rapid corporate expansion, and all promotions were from within the company, so there was a great demand for people to pick up the reins and take charge. I was fortunate and fascinated to watch and learn from people I considered to be masters at both leadership and excellence. I learned that the level of excellence exhibited by any organization is directly proportional to the level of excellence exhibited by those in leadership. Those years ignited a lifelong burning need in me to explore and seek to understand the path to excellence and excellent leadership.

Since leaving corporate life, I've been a camp cook, wilderness hunting guide, hunting guide training school manager, assistant pastor of a church, an entrepreneur who has owned three retail stores, a law enforcement officer, coroner, farm worker, and most recently, a fly fishing guide. In absolutely every occupation and every application, I discovered that true leadership and the pursuit of excellence share the same principles and challenges. I've also found that the benefits experienced by individuals and organizations who pursue and embody excellence are manifold in every single case. The world is still looking for excellence and true leadership, but people have been conditioned to accept less, disappointingly less. When excellence is found, they want it and are willing to pay for it.

People in organizations talk about leadership and excellence. They come up with phrases and shortcuts to tell the world they are going to be excellent or how excellent they already are, but, in most cases they totally miss the mark. If your organization is truly excellent, it will be obvious, everyone will recognize it, and there will be no need to convince anybody that it is. If you're not excellent, you won't fool anybody with your advertisements.

The traditional tried-and-true hard work and attention to detail and the appreciation for the people who rely on us to lead have been disregarded or discounted by those who would want us to believe that there's a magic potion or quick fix that can transform ourselves and our organizations overnight. It seems that people believe that they can convince those they serve of their excellence just by claiming to be great.

I spend a lot of time looking at social media pages for those proclaiming to have the path to leadership and excellence figured out. Too often, they involve catchy sayings to repeat in front of the mirror in the morning to make you feel good about yourself or feel good about your failures. They miss the part about how becoming a true leader and pursuing true excellence requires action and effort, day after day. It requires special people who are willing to take on the challenge to step up and make it happen. A quick review of the operating results of some old traditional companies that fail every year will illustrate what happens when leadership loses focus of the mission, their people, and their customer and becomes complacent. Or as the Nordstrom family used to say, "They decided to let the money guys or the computer guys tell them how to run their company instead of listening to the people who are really out there on the sales floor, with the customer, doing it every day."

You can't convince people you are excellent just by talking about it or by thinking good thoughts. The market decides who is or isn't great based upon its experience. The customers get the final vote, and they vote with dollars.

As a fly fishing guide, I have a real fondness for old, classic, traditional, tried-and-true flies. A perfect example, and probably my favorite, is the Royal Coachman dry fly. This design dates back almost two centuries to the mid-1800s, when Tom Bosworth, a coachman for the English Royal Family, tied the first one. It is as effective today as it was then. It is made from traditional natural materials, feathers, fur, and fiber, and tying one well takes some skill and attention to detail. It's a beautiful fly to look at. It floats naturally, and with proper presentation, will fool the most selective trout. I'm one of the few guides on my river system who still uses that fly, but my clients catch trout, day after day, with the old Royal Coachman.

Modern fly tiers have developed synthetic fibers, UV reflecting dubbing, foam rubber and premade plastic bodies, wings, and legs, and a host of other new and better shortcuts to tie a trout fly. While some modern shortcuts work, there's still something solid, effective, and reassuring about using those tested and proven methods and principles that have been getting the job done for centuries. One day on the river, I was tying on a Royal Coachman dry fly and had this sudden realization that we, as humans, are in such a hurry to discard the traditional ways, and traditional people for that matter, and to improve them just because they're old, without ever considering the value, history, and legacy those ways have and that we lose the lessons those before us already learned.

We need to take another look and capitalize on what's already been proven to work, just like this classic fly that few of us use anymore. Failing companies and mediocre organizations need to go back and relearn the basic proven principles their founders used to build them, back to what made them great to begin with, and reapply them.

Leadership and excellence are exactly like that. The core concepts, materials, if you will, are traditional, proven, and uncomplicated. They've been handed down for centuries, and they don't vary. The rules still apply as well as they always have, and they work. There's no shortcut to greatness in excellence or leadership, and it takes true excellent leadership for an organization to even have a chance to be excellent itself. Hard work, attention to detail, attention to and appreciation for those around you, extreme focus, an insatiable desire for knowledge, and high expectations for yourself and others are just a few of the basic materials that go into it.

There is really no substitute or shortcut. It takes some skill, a willingness to learn, and considerable endurance and patience, along with a commitment to make things happen. As usual, those who are being led get the final vote. People choose to follow great leaders because they are excited to be a part of what they have going on. That really is what it all comes down to.

Here's the good news: Excellent leadership and organizational excellence are still attainable by those who are willing to do what it takes to get there. As I said earlier, the benefits enjoyed by those who pursue them are great.

1
WHY EXCELLENCE MATTERS

"Many men go fishing all their lives without knowing it's not the fish they are after."
–Henry David Thoreau

AS WE CONSIDER THE commitment and energy investment required to attain and maintain excellence in an organization, we have to wonder, where is the payback for this investment? Why does it matter if we are excellent, or could we do just as well being mediocre and have a much simpler time of it? These are valid questions.

It takes a tremendous amount of effort, commitment, teamwork, and cooperation to move an organization up the scale from poor, to mediocre, to decent, to good, and all the way to excellent. What's the point, and who really cares? How do we know if it will be worth the investment in time, money, frustration, and energy?

The benefits are realized by their effects outside the organization and inside as well. These benefits are a direct result of the effects of excellence within the community or environment in which the organization exists and operates, as well as in the organization itself as a result of the internal changes that occur.

I am going to categorize entities as private or public. Private companies operate from a profit motive, while public entities tend to be service oriented, working from a fixed budget that is assigned by some oversight group. Typically, private companies seek to increase revenues while, at the same time, focusing on expense and overhead control, which are often considered mutually exclusive concepts but really are not. As a corporate president once told me, "Good business cures all ills." Expenses are generally measured as a percentage of sales to determine profitability. Simply put, if you sell more without spending more, you are more profitable than you were previously. Corporate stockholders and company owners expect exactly that from those they have appointed to run the company.

Public organizations continually struggle to perform their function, whether law enforcement, public works, record keeping, road maintenance, or whatever, in an environment of fixed or even shrinking budgets and increasing demands. The work volume and need to expend more resources is often variable, being influenced by outside factors such as environment or public whim.

When organizations are perceived as excellent by those they serve, it means that they have the highest possible approval rating relative to the other groups around them performing the same function. Customers are attracted to excellent companies because they understand that their needs will be met in an enjoyable and satisfactory manner. They understand that there is a high likelihood that they will be treated fairly and receive good value for their investment in the product. People shop and buy to satisfy a need. When they believe a certain organization will satisfy that need in a quick, friendly, and painless manner, they flock there to shop. Nobody returns to a place where they leave unsatisfied if they have another alternative that always provides an excellent experience. Obviously, this translates into significant increases in sales and revenue for the company.

With public organizations, the external benefits of excellence are not as straightforward, but, nevertheless, they do exist. Each public administrator has to present periodic budgets for approval by some oversight group such as a city council, county council, etc., which determines the amount of the final allocation of funds. This is then followed by a process of negotiation where the administrator defends the budget proposal while the decision makers try to allocate a fixed amount of resources among multiple similar budget proposals from multiple agency administrators.

The needs of the entity typically fall into two categories: fixed minimum requirements, or those expenses that maintain the minimum level of service necessary to survive; and variable requirements, or those expenses designated to achieve improvements above the minimum or status quo. To simplify, the decision makers pretty much have to give every group the bare minimum; beyond that, they have discretion to allocate the remaining funds. These funds then, in effect, become an investment on the part of the decision makers and their goal is to allocate them to maximize the return on that investment. This is where excellence jumps up and becomes critically important. If the decision makers believe one of the agencies continually performs excellent work, completes their function within the specified time limits, within the budget that has been allocated, in a quality manner, as opposed to another group that does not, they will look much more favorably on the requests of the excellent group.

If the decision makers see that the budget is well spent and the job well done, they have a very easy task of allocating additional funds to that group in the future. Conversely, if they see that the group habitually generates cost overruns and budget extensions, they are very cautious about ever giving them additional opportunities to waste money.

Within the organization, whether private or public, if the employees are well motivated, efficient, and happy, they work well together as a team, and if they are choosing to do their best, it is pretty easy to see that more and better work is going to be done. If we compare this environment to one where team members are unhappy and really don't care about their work or their organization, where they just do the minimum required to keep their job, we can predict that the first group is going to produce much better results.

When every member of the team participates and takes ownership and interest in the results produced by the organization, you have the proverbial best possible scenario to produce more with less. Not only is more output produced, but better quality output as well, which, in turn, generates the benefits discussed earlier in this chapter. Team members are focused on doing their jobs and doing them well, rather than on the drama and distractions so present in organizations where people are unhappy. Except for some sort of significant technological advancement, there really is no other path to increased efficiency and success with limited resources than to improve the productivity of the existing resources.

In the following chapters, we will explore some of the forces at work and will discover that there's no rocket science or secret code. With focus and effort, excellence is attainable within any organization, and the benefits realized by its attainment are well worth the effort.

2
WHY DO WE CARE ABOUT EMPLOYEE SATISFACTION?

"If I fished only to capture fish, my fishing trips would have ended long ago."
–Zane Grey

I ONCE LISTENED TO the president of a great company addressing a group of his employees. He had many good things to say but probably his most important, and revealing, statement was, "If I don't show up for work tomorrow, nobody would likely even notice. If you folks don't show up for work tomorrow, our company will fail. You are clearly the most important people in the company. I'm way down near the bottom of the list somewhere. I appreciate every one of you and the great work you do every day."

The most important resource within any organization is its people. They comprise the members of the team that does all the work. Without them, the organization is unable to function and will fail immediately. Their outlook, interest level, willingness to help the organization succeed, level of motivation or excitement about their work, and overall feeling of satisfaction with their job are the most important factors determining efficiency and productivity in the entity. No amount of plant and equipment improvement can succeed if the people are not involved and invested in the effort to improve and excel. Without the team supporting them, the leaders cannot do the work or perform the function of the organization.

Most of us spend more time involved in our employment than we do in any other single activity. What we do and how we feel about it influences our identity, our personal sense of self-worth, our mood, our relationships with family and friends, and pretty much our whole outlook on the world. It has often been said that "happy employees bring their best effort to work while unhappy ones bring the minimum effort required to keep their job." That saying is absolutely true, and it is necessary for organizations to develop an environment that focuses first on understanding then on improving employee satisfaction as a first step toward improving organizational success. We need to be tuned in to how our employees feel about their relationship with their job and the organization we serve.

As human beings, we are continuously working to satisfy certain "needs." In 1943, Abraham Maslow published his hierarchy of needs theory. It has been a model for many academics as they discuss the concept of motivation. In a nutshell, Maslow believed that all humans have similar needs, and he arranged them in a hierarchy from very basic, at the bottom of the diagram, to self-actualization at the top. Each level of need must be met before the person can move to the next higher level. Happiness and the sense of well-being increase as each level of need is satisfied. Humans in the workplace are driven by these needs to a very great degree, and, until the leaders of the entity understand how this works, they cannot truly understand how employees respond to how well the entity addresses their needs.

Maslow's hierarchy of needs

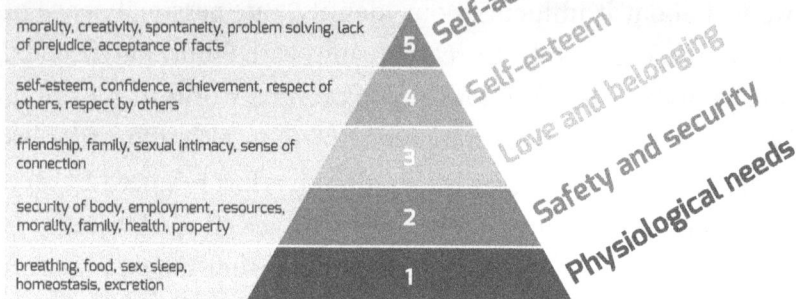

Level	Description	Name
5	morality, creativity, spontaneity, problem solving, lack of prejudice, acceptance of facts	Self-actualization
4	self-esteem, confidence, achievement, respect of others, respect by others	Self-esteem
3	friendship, family, sexual intimacy, sense of connection	Love and belonging
2	security of body, employment, resources, morality, family, health, property	Safety and security
1	breathing, food, sex, sleep, homeostasis, excretion	Physiological needs

If we look at the diagram, we see that as a person goes through life, they are most "self-focused" at the lower levels. If they are starving, they only want to find food; they have no interest in whatever else is going on around them unless it will provide food. Their survival is at stake. As they satisfy each lower-level need, they can then focus on what comes next, the assurance of continued food in the future, for example. As each level is satisfied, a certain amount of stress or fear is removed from their life and they become more focused on the world and people around them. Their feeling of well-being increases as they move up the levels.

As employers and leaders, it is important to understand, at least to some degree, the needs of employees and staff. The basic purpose of employment has traditionally been viewed as "to provide money to buy food, clothing, and shelter." Everybody agrees that we need those things for basic survival. As we take a deeper look, we discover that the job and work environment affect much more.

People need to feel that their income source—their job— is secure and will continue to meet their basic survival needs. People need to belong to, and be accepted by, a group. The work environment is a source for this, along with family, outside organizations, church, sports teams, and other activities. As we look at the hierarchy chart, it is apparent that, after the basic lower-level needs are met, people can move to levels in which their activities have a more positive effect on the organization as a whole. At the upper levels, it is easy to see that people will begin looking for ways to improve the world around them, so to speak, and that mindset, or level of focus, is where employees begin to contribute to the excellence of the organization. They become less self-focused because their basic needs are being met, which enables them to shift their focus toward those around them—coworkers, customers, and the organization itself.

Whether one agrees totally with Maslow, it is easy to see that employees who believe they are compensated adequately and who have reasonably secure employment are relieved of the stress and fear of basic survival. They can begin to focus beyond themselves and their basic needs and begin to look outward to those around them. As they begin to see themselves as an important and appreciated member of the organization, or team, their satisfaction with their work life continues to improve. Conversely, if they believe, accurately or not, that their needs are not being met or they are not being treated fairly, they will tend to find ways to fight the company to force them to treat them better. This may come through union activities, strikes, slowdowns, employee theft, complaining, poor work performance, or many other means.

I'm not trying to oversimplify a complex issue, but hopefully we can see some of the forces at work at the most basic levels of employee motivation. Employee commitment to the team and to the organization is the most important factor in achieving excellence as an organization. Great employees are the most critical requirement for getting there. I also believe that great employees are, more often than not, "made not born" from good employees with good leadership. The organization has to nurture them and bring them to the place where they can become excellent. Most organizations allow their employees to "stall out" or even to go backward from good to mediocre and disinterested. They don't provide an environment for them to achieve greatness.

3
FOCUS

"The solution to any problem, work, love, money, whatever, is to go fishing, and the worse the problem, the longer the trip should be."
–John Gierach

IF YOU GO TO a shopping mall on a busy afternoon, you will be surrounded by crowds of people. Now, find a place to sit and watch these people as they go by. Read their faces, their posture, their body language, and notice what they are noticing. Notice how they react to others. Try to figure out what they are thinking. I've done this hundreds of times and have always found it to be quite interesting. Of course, it helps if you are into watching people. By watching those around us, we can figure out how they relate to others. We can see how they choose to interact. We'll call this "the focus of their attention and action."

Each of us develops our own priorities upon which to direct the focus of our activities and attention. Hopefully over time, our focus will change. We begin life focused on ourselves and our personal needs. Infants are totally helpless, so they make sure that everyone around them knows when they are hungry, wet, tired, or just bored, and they keep informing those around them until their need is satisfied, at which point they sleep until they need something else. Clearly, the focus of their energy is 100 percent inward toward satisfying their own personal needs.

Over time, the infant matures and becomes more capable of tending to its own needs and is expected to begin taking on the role of a family member. This means participating in family activities and, yes, chores. The focus of their energy and effort begins to change little by little to become more "outward" or directed toward the world and people around them. To oversimplify the illustration, eventually the child becomes an adult and, to really make the point here, we'll say a mother with her own family. Now, her energy and efforts become very heavily weighted toward meeting the needs of those around her as opposed to her own needs. Focus then could be said to change with changing life roles and maturity. As people develop maturity, their focus moves from self-centered, looking at their own personal needs and wants, toward a more outwardly directed view that includes the needs and wants of others as well.

Clearly, the priorities vary greatly from individual to individual, and it seems as if some folks never learn to focus on anything other than their own personal needs. How do we evaluate "focus"? Is there a right or wrong focus? We can make the argument that, within the context of excellence, the extreme ends of that pendulum—total focus on self or total focus on others—is not optimum.

This is a complex issue, and I'm just trying to lay out the context since it will be a core issue to the whole discussion of excellence. I believe excellence requires a careful balance of focus and interest. Before any of us can truly focus on others around us, confidence and a belief in one's ability to satisfy basic personal physical and emotional needs have to occur first.

Each of us must know that we are both able to and are successfully providing for ourselves and that our basic needs are being, and will continue, to be satisfied. These needs include not only basic food, shelter, and other physical needs but emotional needs as well. This allows us to move along the continuum of focus to the point where we can now begin to direct our efforts toward the others' needs. If we move so far across this continuum that we no longer tend to our own needs, we eventually find ourselves where we can no longer effectively function and must then go all the way back to self-focus. There's a balance point where we are taking care of ourselves well enough that we have the ability to tend to others too. Each of us must find that balance.

In watching those people at the mall, it is easy to see who is afraid of the world around them and who is comfortable. Sometimes, it's easy to see who is looking to take advantage of or profit from those around them, thereby using others to satisfy their own needs or wants. Those who are comfortable move easily through the crowd, notice those around them, and make eye contact. They might smile or nod at strangers. They seem to spread good feelings to those they contact. It seems that they are "positively focused on and genuinely interested in those around them."

Those who are afraid or worried don't make eye contact. They try not to interact with anybody around them. It's impossible to know why they are afraid, but one could conclude that they seem to believe they will soon be taken advantage of if they interact with the crowd. They have generally no effect on those around them other than to illicit feelings of pity. People who are looking to take advantage of others intimidate those they meet or have a way of making others feel uncomfortable. Humans have a so-called "sixth sense" or "hairs on the back of their neck" that recognize the motivation or intent of those with whom they have contact. We can tell whether others are focused on satisfying their own needs and wants or if they are comfortable with their own situation and thereby focused on the good of others around them.

Now, it begins to become a little clearer. To have a positive effect on others, each of us must first be confident or comfortable with ourselves and our role in our world before we can focus on those around us in a way that has a positive influence. Others recognize and respect a person who is genuinely confident and comfortable with themselves. This person goes through the crowds in life surrounded by a good aura. Their progression of focus from totally inward to totally outward stops somewhere on the outward side of the pendulum, but, to maintain this effect on the world, it is necessary to continually balance between others' needs and our own. To completely neglect either interferes with our personal sense of balance.

Leaders come with many different personalities. Some have a need to control everything and every person around them. Others really have no clue what anybody other than themselves is doing and don't really care to know. Some enjoy being involved in all the details of the lives of their subordinates, never missing a birthday or a child's birthday, always interested in whether somebody is having trouble at home or if something good is happening in somebody's life.

Some leaders key into the emotions and feelings of the people who surround them. Others are so focused on their own life that they have no time for others' lives or concerns. Others are only interested in pleasing their supervisors in their quest for advancement, whatever it takes, with no regard for the effects of their actions on those with whom they work. How we choose to interact, and the intent and motivation of our interaction with those around us, is critical to our effectiveness as leaders.

If we suggest that leadership involves focusing the efforts of subordinates on the organizational mission and of encouraging those subordinates to bring their best effort to the process, then we can conclude that the best leaders are those who others willingly follow and who make others feel good about the process and work mission. Based upon our discussion of focus, it would seem that excellent leaders are focused enough on themselves to ensure that their needs are being met and that they are comfortable with who they are and with their ability to accomplish the task they've been assigned. In other words, they are confident in their role. They are also focused enough on those around them to ensure that others' needs are being met and others are comfortable and confident in their roles as well.

They are focused on others to the extent that they notice how people are doing and feeling and make sure to address others' needs and concerns when they arise relative to their ability and interest to do the job at hand. Effective leaders are confident enough to feel the need to control only that part of their environment that is necessary to control while relinquishing or delegating control to subordinates; in other words, trusting their subordinates to be competent, whenever possible. Their focus is outward when it comes to desiring the best for those around them and extending their efforts toward bringing that to be whenever possible or practical.

As in all discussions regarding motivation, we see that the balance of focus the leader embodies has a direct effect on the feelings of their subordinates. Focus that is in proper balance between inward and outward is necessary to develop an environment of confidence where others choose to come alongside and work at their best level toward the mission with, and for, that leader. Focus that is too much self-centered causes others to naturally be suspicious or concerned about that person's intentions and motives. They are cautious about getting too close to that person and prefer to stay a "safe distance" away.

Focus that is too outwardly directed to the point that one's personal needs are not being met eventually leads to problems that then cause others to disregard or feel sorry for the person. This also leads to group attention being distracted with very little effort directed toward the mission. Eventually, that leader loses effectiveness and becomes the victim of lack of attention to their own needs.

Developing balanced focus is a process. Some people just naturally have it while the rest of us must examine ourselves and intentionally bring ourselves into the correct balance. This necessarily requires us to understand the concept and to visualize how we want to interact with those we wish to influence. As life goes on, we need to continually reevaluate and adjust as the pressures of daily activity exert their influence on us. The true test is how others respond to our leadership efforts.

4
VALUES

"There is no greater fan of fly fishing than the worm."
–Patrick F. McManus

WE ALL HAVE VALUES. They are the rules we live by. They dictate our behavior. Some of us know what our values are, and some of us have never really thought about them but we still have them even if we don't realize it. Excellence requires us to examine our values and to move a few select ones onto, or maybe closer, to the top of our list.

Most of us would say that we value honesty, integrity, and hard work—unless maybe we are in politics. Those things sound good along with ethics, biblical standards of behavior, transparency (as in what you see is who I am, no hidden agenda here), generosity, and compassion. These are all good, of course, and somebody who is trying to live an excellent life should embrace all of them. Here's something else to consider though: How do we know if we are living according to our stated values? We can look in the mirror from time to time and do a self-assessment. "Yep, I told the truth that time when I was tempted not to." "Yep, I did my best on that project."

What do others around you believe are the values you live by? Those we live with and work with see us as we truly are every day and in every situation. They assess our values continuously and have a pretty good opinion of what is important to us and what is not. They know what motivates us and who or what we are trying to be. Their assessment of our values also defines much of how they interact with us and how they respond to us. They don't pay much attention to what we say is important because they can see what we really believe by the lives we live. It is critical that we think about how others perceive us.

Let's look at one blatantly simple illustration of this point. We've all read about the ratings of charitable organizations. Somebody figured out what percentage of some of these organizations' contributions made it to their stated cause. This person also figured out how much the top executives in each organization received in salary and benefits. As a result of this study, it became evident that some of the organizations were keeping most of the money and sending very little of it to the cause they embraced. After this information was published, many people were shocked, surprised, and angry and adjusted their giving, excluding those groups who sent little to their cause.

Why were they angry, and why did they stop supporting those groups? Because people believed they were dishonest and unethical and had a hidden agenda by publicly saying they were compassionate and wanted to help the subjects supported by their organizations; these people now perceived that, instead, these organizations' were secretly collecting what seemed to be an excessive personal profit and benefit from their donors. The original positive response to a perceived "good" value of compassion and helping the unfortunate immediately turned into a strong negative response to the "bad" values of dishonesty, lack of ethics, and perceived fraud.

This process is ongoing all the time. Each of us is surrounded by those we wish to influence—family, coworkers, subordinate employees, supervisors, customers, the list goes on. Those people continuously assess our values and motives and respond to us accordingly. If they feel good about our intent and purpose, they will be comfortable and willing to respond in a positive manner.

If they believe our values are less than good or positive, they will react accordingly by shutting us out or by giving us the bare minimum necessary requirement. We become frustrated and angry with them, and they respond in kind.

The values I listed at the beginning of this chapter are all necessary and critical for anybody trying to live an excellent life, and we must look for and cultivate them daily. We need to put them on our own list of personal values and think about what they mean. There is one more that isn't listed, but I believe it is the most important value for anybody interested in excellence, more so when the excellence involves teamwork and even more so when your role is that of a leader. It is certainly the most rare and difficult value to truly live by in our world: Having a true belief in the value of other human beings.

We must believe that everyone around us is entitled to the same privileges and benefits that we are entitled to. We must find joy in the success of others or at least accept their success as valid. In the case of those who are dependent upon us—family, subordinates, and customers—we must truly believe that we have a duty to assist them in achieving success in their lives. This is hard sometimes. We need to think about this for a minute. What does that really mean?

Does it mean that competition is bad? What if I try to win? No, competition requires doing your best, getting better. Competition is a wonderful thing, taken in proper context, because it challenges each of us to improve, to push our limits, to do our best work. Our society thrives on competition, and it is a great thing. The proper context part is that it does the same for others, and sometimes they win. When that happens, we must genuinely congratulate them and compliment their effort and success. Should we be happy we lost? No, we shouldn't, and we should vow to figure out how they did it and to find a way to improve, then challenge them to a rematch.

What if my neighbor, brother-in-law, or coworker gets a pay raise and now earns more than I do? Our first human response is jealousy. The proper response is to realize that this is a good thing for them and their family and we should be happy for them and step up and congratulate them. I know that sometimes that's hard to do, but we can train ourselves. If we truly appreciate those around us and wholeheartedly believe in their value and worth, it will influence the purpose of our efforts as well. We will actively seek out ways to help others achieve their goals. We will find ways to recognize others for their successes. We will find ways to share the happiness of others or even to give them happiness or satisfaction. How would others around us feel about following our lead if they saw this in our lives and actions?

When we find ourselves in a leadership role, including a parental role, sometimes we fall into the mode of having to control everything and everybody around us, because that allows us to take sole credit for successes. If we allow our subordinates to be right and us wrong or to have a better idea than ours', somehow we feel threatened. How much better would things go if we allowed others to provide input and suggestions or even criticism? How about if we encouraged it? What if they had a better idea? How much better would things be if all the great ideas were on the table for consideration instead of just those of the designated boss?

Obviously, what I'm talking about here requires self-confidence because that's what it takes to let somebody else be okay and competent. By allowing them to do so, and taking it one step further, recognizing them for their great contribution, the whole group succeeds. Every member then becomes a contributor to the success and feels good about it. The boss has an easier job because all of a sudden they don't have to know everything and because the subordinates like them better now. The only thing the boss has to retain is responsibility for making the final decision on the action to be taken and, of course, the credit or blame for the outcome regardless of who contributed the idea. Credit for success is then given to the contributor of the idea as well. I know that's another tough one to do sometimes. We'll explore this further later on.

Does this mean that we become some kind of human doormat who just lets everybody else take advantage of us? Absolutely not. If others have a right to expect good values from us, then we have the same right to expect them from others. We must expect others to be honest, ethical, hardworking, transparent, and to believe in the value and worth of others as well. These things are manifested in behavior, which we can judge or analyze. The person and their behavior are two different things. If a person behaves dishonestly, it's okay to disapprove of that and to respond negatively. You don't have to accept substandard effort from a subordinate employee, and it's important to communicate that, and of course, set the example.

The next, and often overlooked, step that follows though is to turn it around when that person takes corrective action. Recognize and celebrate the corrective action they show you as a result of your communication. We should never accept behavior that reflects poor values. By placing our criticism or disapproval on the behavior—for instance, "I don't like what you did" or "I think there might be a better way to do or say that" as opposed to "I don't like you"—we allow people the opportunity to fix the behavior, their values, and maintain their relationship. By focusing criticism on the person, we destroy the relationship and the opportunity to rebuild or fix things. Sometimes, their behavior and the values they display don't improve and we recognize that people have a choice when it comes to what they choose to do. We can try to influence the choices, but we can't make those choices for them.

This is a difficult subject to put into words. It will be woven into most everything we discuss regarding excellence and motivation. Every interaction we have with others is affected by our perspective on their values, motivation, and behaviors and by their perspective on ours. As humans, we clearly recognize the values held by others because we observe and judge their behavior continuously. If we strive for excellence in our lives and in our interactions with others, we must develop an inventory of values that we will make a part of our lives and we must review this inventory often to see how we are doing.

In our interactions, we need to practice applying those values that we want to reflect. The most difficult, but maybe most important, is a belief in the value, importance, and good of others. As we work on this, we will find that those around us are much more inclined to respond to us positively because they appreciate our focus and the fact that we appreciate them. Nothing guarantees 100 percent success in our relationships, but we certainly have a much bigger influence on how things go than we realize.

5
WHAT DO YOU THINK?

"No man ever steps into the same river twice, for it is not the same river and he is not the same man."
–Heraclitus

WE TOUCHED ON THIS subject earlier, but, in my opinion, the question, "What do you think?" is one of the most powerful questions a person can ask. Additionally, I think it's probably one of the least asked questions in the English language.

Why would we hesitate to ask it? Because it allows the other person to have an opinion that is potentially different from our own. It allows the other person to provide a solution to a problem, potentially different from ours and potentially a better solution than ours. It allows the other person to potentially receive credit for solving a problem instead of our receiving the credit. It illustrates to the other person, and those around them, that they often have the ability to solve their own problems with little or no input from us. It may put a strain on our personal ego.

Why do I say this is one of the most powerful questions we can ask? For the same reasons listed in the previous paragraph! This brings to mind a 1974 *Harvard Business Review* article called "Management Time: Who's Got the Monkey?" When I received my first management assignment in 1977, my former supervisor handed me the article and told me I needed to read it. That was the beginning of a whole new understanding for me. To quickly summarize the principles stated there: As a supervisor, or parent for that matter, the people for whom we are responsible all come across problems and "situations" daily. Human nature is for them to bring them to us, the supervisor, the boss, along with some statement similar to "I'm not sure what to do about this." Human nature for the supervisor is to say, "This is what I think," "Do this," or "Let me think about it, and I'll get back to you."

The *Harvard Business Review* article identifies all these problems as monkeys that, in the beginning, are in the subordinate's care but which quickly jump onto the supervisor's back because the supervisor possesses all of the food and water. Pretty soon, the supervisor has an office full of monkeys that they have to care for and feed while their subordinates have none. If the supervisor effectively teaches their subordinates how to care for their own monkeys, provides the means and training and food and water for them, and refuses to take the monkeys, the subordinates will handle their own monkeys and the supervisor will have more time to do important things that supervisors are supposed to do instead of being overwhelmed with problems that the subordinates could handle.

Obviously, we call this "delegation," and we all believe it is a good idea and makes a lot of sense. If you look around you though, it becomes abundantly clear that delegation isn't all that common. Initially, it takes some extra work since we have to get the others around us used to identifying and finding solutions for their own challenges. Supervisors still feel the need to be in charge—"I'm the boss, so I have to manage stuff and be in charge of everything." Subordinates still oblige the supervisors by letting them handle all the problems.

The guy who handed me that article also said, "The day you come to work and have nothing to do because everybody around you is getting the job done, you are a successful supervisor." And I'm going to add "parent" to this because it applies equally.

I read a commentary on this article, which was written twenty-five years later, in 1999. Steven Covey, in discussing why these principles hadn't become commonplace among supervisors, said, "When they see others gain power, money, recognition, or information, they experience what Abraham Maslow called a feeling of deficiency, a sense that something was being taken from them." He went on to say, "That makes it hard for them to be genuinely happy about the success of others, even loved ones. Many managers fear that a subordinate taking the initiative will make them, the manager, appear a little less strong and a little more vulnerable." He continued, "How then do managers develop the inward security that will allow them to relinquish control and seek the growth and development of those around them? Managers who live with integrity according to a principle based value system are most likely to sustain an empowering style of leadership." In other words, they have to be okay with themselves first, and then they have to value the people around them enough to allow them to succeed too.

It goes back to what we explored previously. Picking from lots of options is bound to provide a better solution than picking from a few. Nobody knows it all, but everybody knows something. A long time ago, I also learned that the people closest to the problem often have the best information.

This whole concept is a process and not an event. It takes a considerable amount of time and repetition to reach the place in a work group or organization where these principles actually begin to happen regularly. The first time I asked an employee what they thought and what they would do differently if they were in my place, they looked at me like my question was some kind of a trick. I had to assure them that I really was interested—no tricks, it's not a trap, ha-ha. We all know everybody has an opinion. The fly on the wall in the lunchroom, locker room, hallway—anyplace subordinates gather—knows they have opinions because they talk about them all the time. And they talk about how we handle problems, pro and con, all the time.

Over centuries of management practices, we have developed the culture that the boss calls the shots and everybody else falls in line, no questions asked. Business schools and academic smart guys talk about delegation and we believe that means "I tell you what to do, and you do it." The boss takes the credit for successes and tries to blame the subordinates for failures. Ego is a powerful force, and an insecure ego is huge.

We are going about it all wrong. The *Harvard Business Review* article and Steven Covey, in his commentary, identified probably one of the most important concepts involved in achieving an excellent organization, or family. We have to actively involve our subordinates in the operation. We need to solicit their opinions and teach them to be a part of what is going on. We need to ask them, "What do you think?" Then we need to shut up long enough to let them answer that question, and we need to sincerely listen to their suggestion because, more often than not, it will have merit.

We need to be able to say, "I like your idea. Go run with it." Then we need to let it continue to be their idea, and we need to give them the credit for both the idea and the success that came about as a result of its implementation. Self-confidence is a powerful force. Some people have it naturally. Most don't. But it can be developed, and supervisors have a tremendous responsibility to nurture this trait in their subordinates. It has been said that "success breeds success." This really means that success breeds the confidence to try again and to take on larger challenges over time.

Confidence grows only as ever more difficult challenges are met and overcome. Competence grows with ability, experience, and confidence. All three have to be present. As successes with recognition come along and as confidence grows, job satisfaction and personal satisfaction grow exponentially. We like to talk about teamwork. This becomes teamwork. The team becomes more competent and skillful. A coach only receives credit when his team is winning. The team only wins when the coach and the players are on the same page, their abilities and skills are improving, they are becoming more competent, and they work together productively. Without everybody involved, it is a dictatorship.

As in previous discussions about excellence, this is not easy. It takes a lot of practice. It's really easy to forget and take the shortcut of throwing out a solution and moving on to the next challenge. Nobody gets it right all the time but, as my old boss said, "The day you come to work and have nothing to do because everybody around you is getting the job done, you are a successful supervisor." The first step is to bring ourselves to the place where we are willing to ask the question and accept the answer.

6
"AND WHATSOEVER YOU DO, DO IT HEARTILY"
COLOSSIANS 3:23

"The man who coined the phrase 'money can't buy happiness' never bought himself a good fly rod."
–Reg Baird

I LOOKED UP THE definition of *"heartily"* in *Merriam-Webster*.com:
- *in an enthusiastic and energetic way: in a hearty way*
- *completely or fully*

Enthusiasm and energy are the key words here. We all recognize those people who approach life with enthusiasm and energy. They shine. They stand out from the crowd around them. They radiate with joy and excitement. Others are naturally attracted to them because they are getting things done. They inspire confidence.

In 1977, I was appointed as project manager for a systems development project. At the end of the two-year system design process, I had to give a presentation to the two co-chairmen of the board, the corporate president, executive vice president, and senior vice president regarding what I believed the system should look like and how it should work. They were to give it a go/no-go vote after my presentation.

The executive vice president was absent during my initial presentation and scheduled a meeting with me the next day. This was in the days when computers in business were relatively new and misunderstood and the management looked suspiciously at the concept of automating what they thought were some of the key roles of their management team. They feared that the supervisors might be tied to their desk looking through piles of computer-generated reports instead of out working with their employees and customers where they belonged. That idea went against the entire grain of the company.

My assigned objective had been to find a way to automate certain tasks, such as bookkeeping, thereby freeing up managers to perform functions that were more important, such as managing their departments by being present on the sales floor. And, by the way, corporate management had voted "no" on two previous attempts to develop a system and had initially told me this was the last time they were going to even look at this idea.

After my initial presentation, I was told they were in favor of moving forward but it must be a unanimous decision among the executive team. So, the final fate of my project depended upon the executive vice president's opinion. I went to the executive VP's office to show him my plan. I was twenty-six years old and had never considered that he might see me as an inexperienced youngster who was trying to influence the company's way of doing business. I knew he was suspicious of computerizing what he believed might be key business functions and that he had very limited understanding of what computerization of these functions even involved. I did feel strongly that I, and the development team, had come up with a very good, and very necessary plan, so I gave him my best presentation.

After I gave him the same pitch I had given the others, he said something I will never forget. First, he looked at me for a while, broke into a big smile, and then said, "Sold by your enthusiasm." I realized that he didn't even understand all of what I had just said, but he believed in me so he was giving the project a yes vote. In the end, the system was developed and implemented and turned out to be a good thing. I got several nice promotions as a result.

I mention this example because it illustrates the result of enthusiasm. I, and those with whom I worked to put this system design in place, put a tremendous amount of enthusiasm and energy into the project. We took personal interest in the product and truly believed it was going to be the key to continued expansion of the company. We knew that it represented a piece of each of us to the rest of the company too. We'd had to define the functions we were going to automate, show that we could do that within the budget we were going to be given, and then proceed in such a way that not only would the top executives believe in our product, but the entire 5,000 or 6,000 employees of the company would believe in it and would support its implementation as well. A backlash there could have killed the whole thing.

As project manager, I was the person most visible and who was the ambassador, but I wasn't the most important person involved in the project. Each team member had a key role. There were technical representatives who knew what we could or couldn't do with the computer, and there were several people who were the project organizers and "timeline watchers." They figured out the series of steps we had to take and how to organize our efforts. They also kept us on track for our schedule and budget.

Several of us went companywide and spoke to every manager several times during the project. We conducted group meetings and individual meetings and worked to make sure we were going to give them a product that helped them, not one that got in their way. We asked them what they needed and how they used information to do their job, then we showed them our ideas and asked for their input. Then we reshowed them until we believed it was the best product. Through this process, they realized we were doing our best to bring them a product that was going to be our best effort to help them with their job. They also realized that we were excited with this design as it came into its final version.

We became convinced that we were developing great ideas and that we were going to present them with a system that would truly solve some of the problems of a growing company. They knew they had input into the design and that we were truly interested in helping them be more productive. We listened to their suggestions then incorporated them into the design of the product. Then we showed them how we had done so and asked what they thought again. We fought the temptation, and, within our group, fought with each other about the temptation to give them all the "bells and whistles" that were available that would just add to the complexity but provide little benefit. It had to be just what they needed, no more and no less. In the end, they had to believe that as strongly as we did, or they would go straight past us to the management and kill the project immediately. We knew there was dialogue happening behind us every day because the company's executive management group was out and about in every facility continuously, speaking to people in every function. They would hear about any doubts.

We were able to develop and implement the system, and it became the basis for improvements and upgrades that continue today. The company is still very successful and was able to expand nationwide as a result of automating these functions.

In the end, the lesson from this is that it worked. We didn't understand all the forces at play then but somehow were able to do it more right than wrong. We were excited about what we were doing, and we were convinced that it was going to be a great thing. As a result, the entire company believed it was a good thing and supported it, even though they had never actually seen it.

I, some forty years later, realize that it takes more than just a good product to achieve success. Those around us probably don't understand everything about what we are doing, but they will watch and listen to us if they believe in us. Immediately, they read how we feel about what we are doing. If we truly strive to bring our best every day to everything we do, to be our best for those around us, if we absolutely believe in what we are doing, they will be more likely to come alongside and support, or even join in our efforts. This whole approach to life, enthusiasm, and energy is contagious and spreads to those with whom we come into contact. Conversely, laziness and negativity will do the same.

Shine in what you do as well as how you do it. Be proud and excited to put your name on your work.

7
"LEAD OR MANAGE?" LET'S REVISIT IT

"Fly fishing for wild trout on quiet waters must be one of the toughest and craziest ways to catch fish ever invented by man, as well as among the most frustrating and humiliating."
–John D. Voelker

THE COMPARISON OF LEADING versus managing is a worn-out cliché, and I risk boring myself by even talking about it because others before me have beat it to death. The interesting thing about this discussion is that, when I look around, I discover it's still something we're not getting right.

In looking at organizations, especially multilevel ones, we can see how easily the efforts of the various groups could get disorganized and fragmented and how the focus of their efforts may not all be aligned. If that is the case, then it is easy to see how organizations can, and often do, reach a state where there is no longer positive forward movement toward "success." Instead, they flounder around like some giant amoeba that quivers and shakes but can't move itself readily along.

Many organizations, and those in charge of organizations, still mistake activity and noise for progress. Activity is necessary for progress, but the mere presence of activity does not mean that progress is being made. The activity of every work group, on every organizational level, must be harnessed and directed correctly before the mission will ever be achieved. The missing piece of this puzzle is somebody who can see and understand the difference and who is willing and able to step in and take charge. Somebody who clearly understands the organizational mission must be in charge of every effort.

If this is such a big deal then why does it still happen? Why don't we just go in there and point everybody the same way? I wish I knew the answer to that. Some sort of force must be applied to all the effort that is being expended and direct it toward the mission. It's like the transmission on a bus. If the big diesel engine is running full speed in neutral, it's going to make a lot of noise and smoke. The passengers and everybody around certainly know there's a lot of energy being expended and something big and noisy is happening. Until the driver shifts it into gear, nobody is going to get to where they want to go.

Organizations are the same, and if we take the bus example another step further, we can see that the engine has to run, there must be fuel in the tank, the windshield has to be clean enough to see the road, the seats have to be comfortable, the tires have to be inflated, and all of the other related tasks have to be completed before the bus can move forward, even when the transmission is engaged. Further, just because there is a driver in the seat who shifts the transmission into gear doesn't mean anybody is going to get to their correct bus stop. The driver must have a map and must understand how to read the map and how to drive the bus to the stops. The driver must know the schedule and how to use a clock to monitor progress through the bus route. In other words, the driver must have studied and prepared in advance. The driver must understand and be able to visualize the mission. Finally, the driver has to actually step out, take charge, and complete the task as designed. Only then can the passengers have a satisfactory experience and reach the conclusion that this is an excellent bus company. And if there are other competing bus companies around, the driver needs to make sure the passengers on our bus are the most satisfied bus passengers in the market, which will allow us to attract less satisfied passengers to our bus from the other buses.

So now the picture is starting to come a little more into focus. I'm going to call the bus driving function "leadership" and the maintenance/preparation functions "management." Many people misidentify management as leadership. We somehow have been led to believe that management is bad and that leadership is good. That's not true. Neither function has a chance of success unless both are present working together in harmony.

Management tasks are those mundane record keeping, paper filing, detailed things that need to be done. They require specific knowledge and training along with organization and attention to detail. Those of us in supervisory roles necessarily spend a certain amount of time preparing and reading budget summaries, memorizing policies and procedures and applying them when needed, approving and filing paperwork, preparing and modifying schedules, planning projects, and completing a hatful of other tasks that allow us, and those we report to, to figure out what we have been doing and how well we are doing it. These tasks ensure that the pieces and framework are in place to allow us to accomplish our mission. They are the logistical chores that keep the bus running—oil and brake changes, overhauls, repairs, etc. They must be done.

Once management tasks are learned and understood, they follow a consistent pattern and flow and can be easily programmed and predicted out into the future. They take a considerable amount of thought and effort but a fairly low amount of ongoing creativity, stress, or uncertainty. Managing the management tasks more or less consists of "checklist management"—*yep, that job is done, move to the next.* Oftentimes, we assign somebody the role of "group manager" and send them off to manage the group. They fulfill all of these management tasks and things seem good. The paperwork is being processed, the schedules completed, payroll is being sent in so people are being paid. The floors are clean and supplies are ordered on time. Efficiency is everywhere. All the pieces are in place for things to operate well. Activity can continue without a pause, but nobody really analyzes the focus of all the activity. Things just go along as they always have, according to the policy and procedure manual.

The leader, on the other hand, has to be the one who looks all the way out to the horizon. The leader has to clearly understand the mission and the chosen route to accomplish the mission. The leader also has to be able to see the progress markers, waypoints, and "bus stops" that make up the overall route to success. The leader is able to understand and track progress and makes the adjustments necessary to keep moving forward as conditions or situations change. They change the policies and procedures if necessary.

The leader never allows the bus to be distracted from moving toward the goal. The leader challenges the status quo continually, searching for a better way. Accomplishing an organizational mission is most often not an event but rather a process, or series of events, that takes the organization along toward its mission. Obviously, if you work for NASA and your current mission is to land a space capsule on Mars, you complete the mission when it lands. Most organizations don't have it that easy. They have the ongoing mission of providing excellent customer service, excellent community service, or some other "state of being" that evolves and changes over time.

Leaders take on the role of not only clearly seeing the mission and the path forward but of bringing others along with them and helping them to see the path as they move forward. Not only do they bring them along, but a good leader makes others want to go along with them as opposed to having no other choice but to get "on this bus." The true leader also recognizes that they are part of a process that involves multiple other essential roles and people that support their role and that it's essential to work in harmony with each piece or the bus won't move.

The leadership role clearly requires the ability to understand the goal, the right goal, which is the organizational mission, to make a plan and monitor the plan, to track our progress toward accomplishing the mission, to adjust as necessary when situations change, and to communicate all of this to those around us who are involved in the task, while causing others to want to come along on the trip. Leadership requires continual reevaluation of the mission itself to ensure it's still relevant and accurate. It requires considerable effort and generates considerable stress and frustration along the way. Without a leader, the effort expended by those involved in the various organizational tasks cannot be directed toward accomplishing the mission. Effort will be expended toward some end and noise will be made, but the result of this may or may not have much to do with actually achieving the mission we are striving to achieve. We would never know if we are moving forward.

Why would anybody want to be a leader then? Actually, not everybody does, nor should everybody try to be one. It requires a substantial level of patience, commitment, creativity, and effort along with the ability to look forward and deal with evolving conditions and often, difficult people. Not every person is cut out to be a leader. People tend to be naturally attracted to excellent leadership and willingly fall in behind to follow what they interpret as good leadership. We recognize it when it comes along, but most don't know how, or, in the end, even want to do it. That's okay because it takes all kinds of people to make an organization work.

Most strong leaders don't like doing the "management" functions that are absolutely essential to the organization. They like the big picture, not the intimate details. They would, and should, rather delegate those functions to others who are better or more interested in them. Most people who are strong "managers" like the predictability and flow of completing those functions and don't like dealing with the uncertainty, drama, and people who the leaders have to deal with. The problem with those of us who are in charge of organizations is that when looking for supervisory candidates, we often look for the person who is most accomplished at performing the task assigned to the work group in question. We make the best salesperson the sales manager, or the best assembler the assembly unit manager. Maybe we need to reassess this practice and ask who shows us the most leadership quality.

Who is it that has the respect and trust of the other people in the unit? Who is it that comes forward with suggestions or questions the way we do things? Maybe they aren't the best detail worker because they don't function best in a detailed role, but maybe they are the right person for the leadership role because they're better with the big picture. If we put them in the lead, they will lead. Then we just have to make sure the "management" process occurs as well, but, even though it's often not their strength, it's easier to teach a true leader to understand and handle some details than it is to teach a detail-oriented person to see the big picture. Often, the leader will delegate the details to those who are best suited to handle them anyway.

As organizations, and those involved in organizations, we must understand a few related concepts. Number one is that every function is important and critical to the success of the organization. None of them can be left out. Those folks who complete and enjoy the administrative and often mundane tasks are equally as valuable to the overall accomplishment of the mission as those who are out on the front line leading the charge. They deserve equal recognition, thanks, and credit, but often they are not the best people to lead the overall effort itself.

Number two is that strong leadership is absolutely essential to move the organization forward along the path toward accomplishing its mission. There must be a true leader at every level and within every working unit to coordinate the efforts toward the overall organizational mission. These leaders must keep their eyes on the horizon and the big picture while seeing to it that the mundane management tasks that allow the organization to continue to function are being performed as well. Number three is that not everyone is cut out to be a leader. And number four is that, the person with ultimate overall responsibility for the organization must possess the leadership skills and the ability to recognize leadership to ensure that this function is continually being performed at all levels and that the organization in total is on the correct path.

It's a proven fact that, absent leadership, or management, the organization will inevitably fail.

8

MANAGEMENT BY WALKING AROUND, IT'S STILL NOT HAPPENING OFTEN

"The great charm of fly fishing is that we are always learning."
–Theodore Gordon

WHAT IS MANAGEMENT By walking around (MBWA)?
"Management by walking around (MBWA)"
Definition:
Unstructured approach to hands-on, direct participation by the managers in the work-related affairs of their subordinates, in contrast to rigid and distant management. In MBWA practice, managers spend a significant amount of their time making informal visits to work areas and listening to the employees. The purpose of this exercise is to collect qualitative information, listen to suggestions and complaints, and keep a finger on the pulse of the organization. Also called management by wandering around.
—Business Dictionary

Management consultants Thomas J. Peters and Robert H. Waterman Jr. used the term in their book *In Search of Excellence: Lessons from America's Best-Run Companies.* The retail company I worked for in the 1970s and '80s practiced this concept continually. At any time of any day, leadership folks, from the chairman of the board, the president, merchandise managers, buyers, regional officers, store management, and everyone in between, would come walking through the workplace. They spent a few minutes with many of the employees who were manning the sales floor. They noticed the floors, lights, ceilings, displays, and activities of employees. They had their finger on the pulse of the company better than most of their competitors had on theirs. It showed up in the success of the company. Typically, our sales per square foot was double that of our competitors.

Most supervisors in America have an extremely hard time doing this. For some reason, once they've "made it to the top," whether that's the top of the organizational chart or the top of the work unit, they don't want to go back to their roots. Sure, there's occasionally talk about getting out there and "visiting the troops," which results in a few visits by executives to some work groups. Once they do that, they somehow feel their dues have been paid, their obligations have been met, and it doesn't happen again for a long time, if ever. I don't understand it because there are huge benefits to the organization and all of its members when MBWA is a regular part of supervisors' routines.

Take a look at a list of challenges supervisors often have with their subordinates: negative attitude toward management, complaining about what management is doing or trying to do, complaining about expectations of management, lack of interest, low production, arguing or angry at each other, lack of understanding of the organizational mission, poor customer service, failure to maintain a neat, clean organized work area, no team spirit, no pride in the organization or their work, an us versus them mentality, even dishonesty and theft.

So, how do we address all of this? The list is overwhelming to most people who are in charge so they often just retreat into their office and "manage stuff" so they don't have to see or hear the negativity. They try to make the performance-related information that goes upstairs look good enough so they can keep their job. They develop ulcers, migraines, and other problems as a result of the resulting stress. Often, their families suffer the consequences of the stress they deal with at work. The organizational environment may take on a little bit of the atmosphere of a school classroom when the teacher isn't there.

To oversimplify this, the teacher needs to go back into the classroom, so to speak. Even if the supervisor were to walk through the work area and say nothing at all to anybody there, things would be better. The more frequent the walkthrough, the better things would be on the average. People who know that somebody is paying attention do a better job than people who know that nobody is really paying attention—translated, nobody really cares. Then if during the walkthrough that same supervisor spent three minutes talking to each employee about what they were doing, he or she would have a better idea about who understands their job and who doesn't.

Now, if that supervisor spent three more minutes with each employee and asked them how they would like to change the way they do what they do, he or she might find out that the employees have some good suggestions. While this process is happening, the atmosphere in the work group will be changing. Initially, the workers are going to wonder what's going on. They will be suspicious about why this is happening all of a sudden and will be hesitant to really say what they think when contacted by the supervisor. Most of them will be interested; some will not. This may be an uncomfortable situation in the beginning, and some people are going to say things that are unpleasant or unwelcome. The supervisor is going to feel unwelcome for a while and may have to accept, and agree with, some criticism and complaining. Who in the world volunteers for that? In time though, it will become "the way we do things around here."

Now that this process has started, what if the supervisor picked a couple of the subordinates' suggestions and implemented them? While doing that, what if the supervisor actually called a meeting of the work group, brought the people up front who made the good suggestions, thanked them for the good ideas, and announced to everybody where the ideas came from and how they were going to start using them? Next, if time allowed, how about if the supervisor regularly spent some time working out in the work area with or around the subordinates?

Fast-forward. Now that the supervisor has made a regular practice of spending frequent quality time in the company of their subordinates, time that includes working alongside them while they are doing their job, a lot has changed—for the better, I might add. The supervisory person now will know clearly which subordinates want to be on the team and which do not. They will know which know and understand their job and who needs more training and direction. They will know what people are unhappy about and what they like and what they understand or misunderstand about the overall organization and its mission. They will have an opportunity to listen to, and implement, good ideas from the people who actually do the real work and to encourage those people to continue to work toward improving the processes.

Further, the supervisor will discover, understand, and have an opportunity to address misunderstandings, rumors, and misinformation that travel through all organizations from time to time. As time goes on, the subordinates will understand that the supervisor is really interested in them and how they are doing and is working to better understand their life as employees here. An atmosphere of teamwork will begin developing, and production will improve while drama and dysfunction will be dramatically reduced. The supervisor will have opportunities to model good work habits and the organizational mission to those in the work group. They will also be able to address and resolve complaints and dispel rumors while they are beginning, rather than waiting until they are long-lived, developed, and entrenched and exponentially more difficult to resolve.

Additionally, communication will improve with the ongoing opportunity to discuss what the organization is doing and why. The overall stress level within the unit will decline dramatically while production improves dramatically. Job satisfaction will improve. Leadership will begin to replace mere management. Soon, the supervisor will be able to see which employees display leadership qualities that should be developed for future promotional opportunities.

Not only should the supervisor spend time visiting with employees, but, in customer-related industries, they need to spend time visiting with customers. How often do you go to a restaurant and the manager stops by your table, maybe pours another cup of coffee or water, and asks you how your meal is going, how is our menu, or how is our staff doing? What if you were shopping for clothing and the store manager stopped by and asked what you thought of the store, selection, or employees? Customers appreciate that, and the supervisor is allowing those customers to provide suggestions that may improve the success of the business in the future.

This all sounds great, so why doesn't it happen? The supervisor has a lot to do. They have to organize their time and prioritize. But, they also have to recognize that, no matter how much they think they have to do, nothing is more important to the organization's success than them spending at least some regular quality time with their subordinates. They must spend time with their subordinates often, not just when it's convenient. They must be willing to consider and accept criticism and suggestions when they are appropriate and to allow others to be right or have the best idea. Without that, they will fail as truly excellent leaders. They must be willing to immediately address problems that they see and to resolve them. People expect that as part of leadership.

Additionally, poor employees will be quickly identified, and once they are identified and counseled, they may have to be removed from the work group to remove their negative influence. This is very unpleasant but absolutely essential to the overall good of the organization. In other words, it is much harder to be an excellent leader than it is to be a mere manager. Oftentimes, the manager makes the same money and enjoys the same benefit as the person who is putting in the effort to be a great leader. In the long run though, the informed, involved leader achieves greater success, has a better functioning work group, and happier, more productive subordinates. It's a matter of what you are willing to settle for in your own life.

Personally, I believe that MBWA is a lost art but so very essential if an organization is ever going to be excellent. I also believe that, without the very top executive's support, and their participation as well, this won't happen and the organization won't be excellent, ever.

9
WHAT KIND OF EXAMPLE AM I SETTING?

"Who hears the ripple of rivers will not utterly despair of anything."
—Henry David Thoreau

LEADERSHIP, BY DEFINITION, MEANS to lead, show the way, and set an example. When people are new to an organization, they look around at everything going on, listen to all the talk, and investigate for themselves in an effort to understand how things work here, the organizational culture. The impressions they receive from this process far outweigh the information they receive at the new employee orientation class or what they read in the mission statement by the front door. People want to fit in and be accepted, so they work hard to be like those around them in how they think, act, and work.

From time to time, somebody comes along who has a personal standard of performance that exceeds the norm and who applies that standard to everything they do regardless of how those around them approach their tasks. This person usually experiences peer pressure to take it easy, don't make us look bad, what are you trying to prove. Conversely, a person who is performing below the standard or norm will usually experience pressure to pick it up and quit slacking because "we're not going to cover for your poor performance." Generally, one of three things happens: They eventually get tired of being different, so they match their effort to the "standard." They ignore those around them and continue to do what they do, the way they do it, in spite of the pressure. Or, they leave and go somewhere else.

How does the "generally accepted way of doing things here," the organizational standard or culture, come to exist? Those who are involved in the organization will follow the example and the standard set by those who are ultimately in control of the organization. The business owner, CEO, president, chairman of the board, chief, whoever the top person is, must ultimately set the example and lead by the same standards they wish to have in place throughout the organization. In their dealings with employees, customers, and other entities, they must exhibit the qualities, values, and level of service they expect the rest of the organization to embody. Their work product must be as good as or better than that which they require from everybody else.

It's a multipronged sword. First, the leaders must work and interact in the manner which they expect from everybody else. Second, they must demand that same level of effort from their subordinates. Third, they must be in touch with what is happening organization-wide to ensure the others are living up to the standard. Fourth, they have to communicate and enforce this religiously, every day. The big surprise is that it's really hard work and requires a tremendous amount of commitment. The benefit is that, in the quest for excellence, the standards and values exhibited by all who are part of the company become the norm and high standards and excellent values lead to the path to excellence in everything else that happens within the organization. It's part of the basic foundation for excellence, without which there will never be excellence.

The moment the leadership takes a shortcut or does something other than what they request from the rest of the organization, those around them will notice it and it will become news on the organizational gossip tree. The people in the organization will recognize that there seems to be a double standard in place, which will cause them to lose respect for the leadership and for the standard that is being requested or required for everyone except the leadership themselves. Organizational pride will suffer, and standards will begin to erode to match the level displayed at the top.

I find it interesting that oftentimes, those in leadership roles fail to realize how much others within the organization pay attention to their actions. As a leader, we effectively live in a fish bowl where everyone around us can, and does, watch, analyze, and discuss whatever we do. They get to know us very well and soon clearly understand how we feel about our job, the overall organization, the products we produce or function we perform, our customers, and subordinates. They know who our favorite people are and who we dislike. They also understand our values and ethics, our expectations for ourselves and for them, and our level of interest in being a great leader. No matter what we say or preach, they clearly see what we really mean and expect based upon our day-to-day interactions with them. Then they learn to match their approach, values, and attitudes about their work to the example we've shown them.

We become the "norm," the standard that defines the culture and personality of the organization we lead. Looking at the work group will, inevitably, be like looking in a mirror at ourselves. They will reflect what they see in us. Hopefully, we like what we see when we look around. If not, it's time to set a better example.

Only when the leadership of the organization displays, and requires, excellence will the rest of the organization display excellence. I'm afraid our culture has spawned the idea that once we make it to the top we can surround ourselves with our friends and hang out doing important stuff that we don't have to tell the rest of the organization about. If we write enough rules and policies for everybody else to follow, the job will get done. Meanwhile, the rest of the organization receives no clear example of expectations, so the organizational culture, the "way things are done here," evolves in spite of the leadership plans. Middle management ends up trying to figure out for themselves what is tolerated by the upper management and how to get their subordinates to do it. The system is inefficient, and excellence is nowhere to be found.

The common theme in all of this is that excellence has to be something the very top leaders truly want in the first place, and they have to want it bad enough to do the work it takes to get there. Excellence is an uncommon attribute because it requires a special person to be willing to do what it takes.

To go back to the essence of the title of this chapter, the entire organization will follow the example set by those in charge.

10
HOW GOOD ARE YOU WILLING TO BE?

"The act of fishing transports us to a special world, and a state of mind, where we are free."
–Fennel Hudson

WE ALL LIKE THE sound of the word "excellence." It makes us feel good, brings up feelings of respect and admiration for those who wear that label, and makes us ponder what it means to be excellent. Most of us would like to be excellent, but few actually ever get there. In our society, the states of "mediocre," or maybe "advanced mediocre," have become what we've learned to accept and expect. "Good enough" isn't so bad to us because, after all, it's "good enough" and we are often surrounded by "bad."

Who decides who or what is or is not excellent? Who sets the standard? Because of our own personal prejudices, ego, and insecurities, we cannot accurately see how we stack up to the standard. Those who benefit from the services or actions we provide make that decision. I can never truly tell if I am excellent or not because, obviously, I am biased.

Many people and organizations promote excellence. We hear it regularly in advertising and political campaigns. My observations have proven over and over that those who promote their own excellence are often not excellent. That doesn't mean you shouldn't desire to be your very best and to continuously improve or that you shouldn't communicate your desire to be excellent. A profound humility is one of the primary qualifications of people and organizations that are trying to get there, and typically those who boast of being better than everyone else often display an overfed ego rather than a true desire to be excellent. Another qualification is a strong work ethic and an infectious need to help and involve those around you to see, understand, and to work toward achieving the vision of excellence that you hold for yourself, for them, and for the organization.

Recently, I spoke to a CEO who was attending an event in which I was participating. A local unit of his organization was working with a community group to promote partnerships between the organization and local citizens. I told him it was nice to see him in attendance and it would be good to see him more often. He told me he has probably been around to visit with about 60 percent of the work groups since he became CEO, two years before. I told him the local group had been waiting to see him but I guess it just hadn't worked out yet.

While I had the CEO's attention, I decided to take another step. I said, "It would be great if you and your staff came out and spent some time with all the units once in a while." He said, "I spend some time with the union groups." I added, "If you folks came out on occasion and spent some extra time with the various crews, you know, maybe even worked a little alongside them, I bet you would learn a lot and so would they." He said, "Whenever we come around, people look at us like they wonder why we are here." He changed the subject and suddenly saw somebody else that he needed to speak to. What he failed to say was, "When we come around, people ask us questions and make suggestions about how we could do things better, and that makes us uncomfortable so we just limit who we actually speak to." What he also failed to say was, "I'm not willing to make the commitment to be an excellent leader."

Excellence is hard to attain. It requires contact—lots of contact. It requires contact by the top leadership with every other member of the organization and contact with all the people who hold leadership roles. It also requires contact with customers or those served by the organization. The contact must be frequent and continuous so that the ideas, vision, and ideals of the organization get communicated and reinforced from the very top to the very bottom.

Additionally, excellence requires self-assessment, which means soliciting feedback from those that are being served, whether customer or subordinate. That takes humility and thick skin. Criticism and suggestions are huge learning tools, but they are also painful. People who don't solicit ideas and constructive criticism will never accomplish true leadership or growth. There must be a continuous search for opportunities to get better. A true leader says, "I don't have all the best ideas. My role is to search out the best ideas and apply them to our organization and to recognize and reward those who supply these ideas so they will be encouraged to continue finding new and better ones." The leader will never know everything about anything, but a true leader will be the person who encourages others to continue to improve and bring their best to the table. The leader never rests in the quest to find a better way and never allows those he or she serves to rest either. I read something that said, "You will never achieve perfection but along the way you will arrive at excellence."

What prevents excellence? In leaders, I believe the primary roadblock is ego and pride. So often, we believe this self-talk: "If I allow others to be good or better than I am, it will reflect poorly on me." "Everybody must see me as the source of the success of our organization if I am to continue to receive the credit." It's funny, because that's the exact opposite of the true formula. The leader who brings out the very best in every member of the organization, who recognizes and rewards those who try and encourages more of the same, will lead a growing and blooming organization. They are not limited by their own capabilities but tap into the resources and ideas available organization-wide.

Laziness and willingness to settle is the other limiting factor. We have learned to accept mediocrity. Often, we use the term "good enough." What does that mean? Good enough for who? That expression, by definition, leads to the conclusion that it could have been better, but it apparently meets somebody's lower standard so we can live with it. To go from "good enough" to "great" usually requires a significant amount of effort, time, and perseverance that most people are not willing to invest. Hence, excellence is again some concept out in the distance. We either put in the effort to be great or spend our time justifying our lesser level of performance as "good enough" for somebody somewhere.

It comes down to a personal standard and a choice each of us must make daily. How good am I willing to be? It applies to every task and every situation. I'm not saying I have to be excellent every time. When I mow the lawn or fry an egg, sometimes I'm happy with "good enough." When I work for somebody else or provide a service for somebody else, I want it to be excellent because I would expect the same in return. When I teach my children or grandchildren, or work with my professional subordinates, I try to emphasize and demonstrate excellence in the hope that they will learn to understand it and run with it as a life goal for themselves as well. It really is very hard work if it's done right. There is no rest, shortcut, or down time, but the final result is worth it.

Who decides if it's excellent? The recipients and beneficiaries of the effort will tell you . . . if you are brave enough to ask, of course.

11
SURROUND YOURSELF WITH THE BEST PEOPLE

"Rivers and the inhabitants of the watery elements are made for wise men to contemplate and for fools to pass by without consideration."
–Izaak Walton

AN ORGANIZATION IS MADE of its members. There are many roles to fill, each of which has unique and varied requirements. Each of these is carried out by people. The saying that goes, "The whole is greater than the sum of its parts" applies equally to organizations, as does "The chain is only as strong as its weakest link."

The CEO of any organization may be an insightful, creative, hard-working person, but the CEO only does one job. Everything else happens because of somebody else's efforts. Recruiting, hiring, and training are the most important processes in any organization. Only the very best people will produce the very best product. I was the internal affairs investigator for a sheriff's office for a while. During a training session, I heard a presenter say, "An employee who is a problem in the beginning of their career will likely still be a problem twenty years from now." In over forty years of supervision, I have found that to be true. I believe the single most important step in the organizational process is hiring.

Before the first employee is hired, those who are involved in this activity must understand and define what they are going to require. It is helpful to prepare a list or some written description of the desired traits that will define the best possible employee. It is just as important to have a list of disqualifying items. These traits can be categorized into groups—those that must be present, those that are highly recommended, and those that would be nice to have. For example, honesty, integrity, strong work ethic, and ability to work as a team member would be absolute requirements, while specific fields of education, previous related experience, or where the candidate resides may be advantages or may present challenges the organization will have to overcome but would not necessarily mean the candidate would not be a great employee. Any history of dishonesty, failure to get along with others, laziness, or inability to stay with employers would certainly be a red flag and should set off warning bells, requiring further critical investigation.

All along, we have discussed how excellent organizations must have excellent leadership that promotes excellence in every way. We have spoken about how excellence only happens when leadership sets the example and spreads it to every level of the organization. The other half of that equation though is that, as the members of the organization are exposed to the leadership, they must then buy into the idea of excellence and follow the example and work to the level of the expectations that they are being shown. I would venture to guess that less than half of the potential employees who drop applications in the hiring box would be willing to do that.

How do we find those people? The first step is to have clearly defined expectations for employees. These expectations embody the idea of excellence and are presented to candidates right up front in the form of mission, vision, and value statements. If these are right at the top of the employment application, it sets the tone for the rest of the process. Many organizations now have an online application process where candidates fill out electronic forms, submit them electronically, and are notified electronically.

Meanwhile, there is no substitute for face-to-face contact and a good interview. Reference and background checks are critical. We all want to be politically correct and are so afraid to offend somebody that we tiptoe around these issues, but we should not. I attended a number of interview and interrogation classes as a law enforcement officer. I learned that face-to-face interviews result in a very good awareness of whether the interviewee is being truthful, deceptive, or is just uncomfortable with the subject matter being discussed. It isn't necessary to "interrogate" potential employees, obviously, but paying attention as they answer questions as well as paying attention to how they answer and what they don't answer will tell you as much as the answers themselves.

Always remember, the person sitting in front of you wishing to become a member of your organization left a job, or several jobs, somewhere else. That may be because they thought they could better themselves working for you, or it may be because they couldn't get along with the people or work up to the level of expectations where they were before. In the latter case, they won't tell you that and the previous employer is afraid of being sued so they won't tell you that either. It is on you, the person responsible for hiring, to figure these things out before you hire this person. They could be a great asset or a huge liability, but remember, once you hire them, they are going to be with your organization for a long time.

Take the time and ask the right questions, do your homework up front, and save the company the heartache of having a weak or poor employee in the pool. After a first interview, you may decide you saw or heard some things that need to be followed up or investigated further, which is normal. If so, do it before you commit to hire that person. I've learned to listen to my first impressions and always listen to that little voice in the back of my head. Spend as much time as necessary to satisfy the questions or concerns that come up during the interview. Do not be afraid to ask difficult questions. Problems that are missed here will always resurface later, after the employee has been hired. It's okay to say, "Thanks for coming in. I'll think this over and get back to you later."

Maybe a follow-up interview is a good idea. Sometimes, having another person sit in on the follow-up interview will help identify whether your concerns were justified or only imagined. When you are satisfied that you have the information you need to make an informed decision, then move forward. Patience is certainly justified when selecting employees. If you have to go through a hundred candidates to find that great "one," then do it. This will pay off over and over during their potential decades-long career with your organization.

Energy, attitudes, and interest are contagious. A group of happy, motivated employees will do tremendous things. If you throw a lazy, sourpuss person into the mix, this will negatively affect the whole group and the whole group will become unhappy because of that one negative influence. They expect leadership to prevent or remedy that situation; the bad employee challenges leadership to do something about them. They know it is difficult to remove them once they become entrenched. Good employees appreciate the value of good coworkers and expect and appreciate leadership that hires good people. Great people are proud to be a part of a group of great people.

Probationary periods are a great tool as well. Every employee must be made aware right in the beginning that we are happy to have them here but that their continued employment is conditional, depending on how things go during a probationary period. In the event that it appears they and the organization are a poor fit, they can be removed for any cause during that period. The probation should be at least a year so any "honeymoon period" during which the new employee is exhibiting their best, but not truly characteristic, behavior will have time to be over.

People are good at putting on a performance when trying to influence others but only have the energy to maintain the performance for so long. Eventually, their true self shows up. If that true self is what we are looking for and what we thought we hired in the beginning, good news! If that true self is someone other than who we were hoping for, then the probationary period allows us to correct the mistake before it becomes entrenched.

Related to this is an absolute need to make clear, unbiased evaluations as the probation goes along and to identify and take action whenever it appears the employee is not working out. Oftentimes, those doing these evaluations feel sorry for the probationary employee or choose not to be the bearer of bad news, so they fail to identify, or they understate, weaknesses or problems. This can be catastrophic, and people need to realize that this is a business decision, not a place for personal feelings. They also need to understand that only by identifying these issues can they be addressed and the employee potentially counseled and brought around to an acceptable level of performance. The evaluators must also realize that, by misidentifying a poor employee as a good employee, their organization could end up with this poor employee as part of their company, driving down morale, performance, and satisfaction for decades. It sounds harsh, but it can't be any other way. Poor employees must be removed.

Counseling is appropriate for poor employees but, if things do not resolve themselves, then the employee is not going to work out, period. I've always said, "People either change or they won't change." If people do not respond immediately to counseling then don't expect them to do so later. Great employees want to be great, and they work on getting better when given a chance. When given suggestions that will help them become better, they accept and implement the suggestions immediately.

I'll just touch briefly on compensation. I once worked for a great company. They paid more than their competitors and were straight-up honest with their employees. They said, "We pay more than anybody else because we expect our employees to be better than anybody else's." They expected a lot and wouldn't settle for less, but they were willing to pay for it. The result was that the benefits improved their bottom line. It was a great investment.

In summary, hiring is the most important process in any organization. An organization is only as excellent as the people who work there, and excellent leadership is only effective if there are excellent subordinates who want to pick up the ball and run with it. Weak employees spread that weakness to the people around them.

During the hiring process, it is mandatory that the person doing the hiring communicate clearly the values, attitudes, expectations, and requirements that are necessary in the members of the organization. These should be documented to remove any question regarding what they are. The background check and interview are key to finding out what happened in this candidate's past that resulted in them making an employment change. Before any hiring happens, those doing the hiring must have a clear understanding of the qualities that make up an excellent employee as well as those that disqualify an employee. If we do our due diligence and try to hire the very best, and, if after their probationary period the employee is what they appeared to be, the organization will be a better place because they have added a great new member. Those doing the hiring will have accomplished their mission. The employees are the foundation upon which excellence must be built. It really is that important.

12
EXPECTATIONS

"I imagine no art has ever been learned from books, fly-fishing is no exception."
–G.E.M. Skues

BRIEFLY, MY WIFE AND I took on the responsibility of caring for a child who had come from a dysfunctional family and had been in the foster care system for three years. We were involved with this child, an eleven-year-old girl, for six months before she moved on to a new, hopefully permanent, family. In her school, the grading system was one to four, with one being "fail" and four being "excellent." Just prior to our taking custody of her, my wife attended a parent teacher conference with her teacher and the then-foster mother. The teacher told them that this young girl was averaging 1.5 in her subjects and that she had serious problems with math especially. She added that the main problem was poor work quality, focus, staying on task, and work not turned in, and that she was definitely a bright girl who was not working anywhere near her potential.

My wife and I were amazed that this situation even existed for a child who was in fifth grade and who, for a number of months, had been the only foster child in the home where she was currently assigned. My wife voiced her displeasure and concern to the teacher and foster parent, only to be told by the foster parent, "You have higher expectations." No kidding. Yes, thank you very much, we expect those around us to perform at the level of their ability. We expect no less than their best effort, not always "fours," but their best effort.

Over the last few months of the school year, we spent time with the girl, reinforcing the concept of doing your best, not with threats and real rewards (bribes), but by congratulating her when she worked up to her potential. We helped her where she needed help but refused to do her work for her. We talked about her school responsibilities at the end of each day. At the end of the year, two and a half months after the conference, she received an award for being the most improved student in her school and her grades averaged three to 3.5.

This young girl's success had nothing to do with us being special or experts or anything else, but was completely due, first of all, to her being a very bright girl, as the teacher had advised us. Second, it was due to her being aware of our expectation that she would do her very best in all she did and us reinforcing that every day with encouragement and congratulations as she experienced successes and counseling her when she was slacking. Now that she has moved on to a new living situation with another, hopefully permanent, family, our prayer is that she takes this one lesson with her through life.

In our world, people are willing to accept mediocrity. Good enough is good enough in most cases, and we've become a society where everybody is supposed to be nice and nobody is allowed to say things to others that may make them unhappy or uncomfortable. Somebody came up with the idea of "participation trophies" because it wasn't nice to reward just the winners and make the losers feel bad about themselves. We carry this attitude with us in our families, jobs, and through all of the contacts we make in our daily lives.

The other side of the discussion regarding expectations is that, sometimes expectations are set too high. This is probably most visible in youth sports. Having had children who participated in sports, it astounded me how some parents could never be satisfied with their child's performance nor with the coach who never gave their child a "reasonable chance" to show how great they were. These folks, it seemed, would never be satisfied until their child had a full ride scholarship to college and maybe even a pro sports career. Apparently, it never occurred to them that their child might not have been physically at that level of athletic ability or might, in fact, have not been that interested in this sport to eat, drink, and play it twenty-four hours per day.

These parents fumed, argued, and walked around angry and obsessed with their child's performance and position on the team. They criticized their child publicly for what they considered to be unacceptable performances and criticized the coach because their child wasn't a star yet. No amount of effort on the part of the child seemed to be enough to satisfy them. Many youth sports coaches love coaching the kids but can't stand the parents, so they quit coaching.

This attitude spills over into many areas of life.

We've all worked for bosses who thought, *If I ask for the sun maybe I'll get the moon,* meaning they believed that by asking for more than subordinates could possibly accomplish, the subordinates would somehow be able to actually do more than they would have otherwise. Given this, we all understand the difference between reasonable and unreasonable expectations. Most of us have a level of expectation for ourselves that we believe to be reasonable. Now, I also believe we often set our expectations below our actual ability but, for today, we know what we believe to be a reasonable expectation. We are willing to accept that expectation of us from others because we believe it is reasonable. If somebody, especially somebody of influence, says they expect more than we truly believe is reasonable, especially if they demand more, we don't like it, in fact we probably become angry. For sure, we discount their expectation as unreasonable, impossible, and we probably lose respect for them and their leadership ability in the process. Generally, we have very little motivation to accomplish whatever it is that they say they expect us to accomplish.

My focus in this chapter is on reasonable expectations—reasonable, but I might add, challenging. As people overcome challenges, their confidence increases as does their belief that they can take on, and overcome, even greater challenges. Over time, their expectations for themselves become higher. Good leaders understand this and help their subordinates see and understand what is happening and continue to raise the bar little by little as their confidence grows. Notice that when I was discussing the girl we had temporary custody of, I said, "We expect no less than their best effort, not always 'fours,' but their best effort." Initially, she saw herself as a 1.5 student, but over time, as she did better on a few assignments, she began to realize she was capable of more than she initially believed. She went from 1.5s to 2s, to eventually 3s and 3.5s. Had we said initially, "We won't accept anything below a three on your work," she would have become angry and demotivated because she believed it was impossible. She had to grow into it, but she was excited to receive that award because she knew she earned it and deserved it.

As in everything else we have discussed related to excellence in leadership, you cannot expect those you lead to ever go beyond the example and level of effort you are willing to show them day by day. The expectation applies equally to the leader and everyone else in the group. We jokingly say, "Do as I say, not as I do," but that is not a joke, and excellent leaders know that those they lead are expecting them to set the example and place the bar at the level they want others to work to achieve. As in everything else we have discussed, the leader must make expectations clear and discuss and reinforce them continually. Continuous, ongoing encouragement and recognition for the efforts and successes of those around them are necessary if the group is to continue to move toward the goals. Those who are falling short need to be counseled, trained, and pushed to move forward at the expected pace.

As we saw in a previous chapter, those who cannot or will not live up to the reasonable expectations need to be relocated or removed, or they most assuredly will slow down the whole group. People believe in fairness and won't accept a higher expectation for themselves than is applied to those around them. The expectation has to apply to everybody or else it applies to nobody. Sometimes, it's not so nice, but it is absolutely necessary to expect the very best effort from those around you and to settle for no less. Participation trophies were a stupid idea, even to those who received them. Everybody knows that only the best effort should be rewarded even if they don't complain when they receive a reward for less. In sports and other games, the winner receives the reward, the others don't.

In life, those who do their best need to be recognized and rewarded and those who don't need the encouragement to step up or to move on to another situation. People have an ingrained sense of right and wrong and they know this to be true, and intuitively expect it, even though our society wishes it weren't, so nobody gets their feelings hurt. It's not a number score. It's a mindset and level of effort, and it's a matter of asking, "Is there something else I can do that would make things better?" Cowboys have a term for that: "try." If a cowboy says his horse has a lot of "try" then you know it's going to be a good horse. He may not be achieving every goal he sets out to accomplish yet, but he puts his best into every effort and doesn't quit just because he's a little tired.

In summary, it is necessary to have the highest expectations for ourselves and those around us. We should never be willing to accept good enough if something can be better. Those in positions of leadership—parents, bosses, mentors, and others—must set the example by expecting and exhibiting their personal best in the tasks they take on. They must also expect, communicate to, and encourage their subordinates to aspire to do their best and to accomplish great things daily; and they must recognize and congratulate the effort they see. These expectations must always be tempered in reality and reasonableness because people will aspire to achieve goals and expectations that they see as challenging but possible, but they will become angry and demotivated if pushed to reach levels they believe are impossible.

As in every other aspect of leadership, helping others achieve their best requires daily effort and focus on the part of the leaders. And notice that the most important thing to talk about is the expectation regarding the level of effort and "try," not their level of achievement. Achievements are important, and they will come in time if the level of effort is there. Focus more on the try than the end result.

13

A CULTURE OF GROWTH AND A VISION FOR THE FUTURE

"The finest gift you can give any fisherman is to put a good fish back, and who knows if the fish you caught isn't someone else's gift to you."
−Lee Wulff

TO SURVIVE AND GROW, all organizations must be continually looking to the future. Society, the environment, our competitors, the marketplace, even our own organization continually change and evolve. This process is inevitable, and we need to see it, understand where it is going, and make adjustments to address change as it occurs if we hope to survive and prosper. This is why so many "old-line" organizations just fade away. They reach a peak, achieve some success, then sit back to congratulate themselves and enjoy it while the world changes around them and they become irrelevant and fail to survive. All the time, those in leadership ask themselves, "What just happened?" because they missed the changes. So, what did happen? Their processes and people stopped changing and evolving to keep pace with the world around them the day they decided they'd made it to the top.

People in sales organizations sometimes have an easier time understanding this concept. In my late teens and early twenties, I was a salesperson who received a percentage of my sales as commission. No matter how well I did today, I always started back at zero tomorrow morning. Each day involved building sales one by one, customer by customer. To be competitive, I had to continually improve myself and continually find ways to get better in order to make a living and keep my job. The idea presented here is critical to understand for everyone who aspires to be an excellent leader. As a salesperson, **I enjoyed success, but I would not achieve permanent success if I sat back, relaxed, and enjoyed today's success because I would immediately stop generating any future success.**

So, what does this have to do with leadership? Excellent leaders understand this concept. They understand that their efforts, focus, and interest must always be primarily upward and forward. Glimpses to the past are necessary to relearn the lessons that were there and to review the challenges that have been overcome, but the important things are not there and really aren't around today either. We can be pleased with our successes, but we must understand they are temporary. Leaders are not the people who have their nose buried in the policy and procedure manual to make sure nobody breaks a rule or forgets to dot an I or cross a T. Leaders actually challenge the rules and procedures as they relate to the overall well-being of the organization and as to their relevance to the overall path toward the mission.

Leaders must identify and recognize the changes and trends around them that will affect their organization. They recruit the assistance of others and gather information from multiple sources. They have the ability to see the big picture and to project the organization's path. This enables them to see the challenges and adjustments that need to be made today to affect tomorrow's successes. In a company I worked for, we had a concept called "shopping the competition," which involved spending considerable time in the establishments of each of our competitors. If we discovered they had a good idea or a good product we had somehow missed, we copied them and tried to make it better. Every day, we feared that somebody was going to discover a better way and our customers would like them more than they liked us.

The leadership of the company said, "We're going to make this simple. We will never have a big, thick policy manual, but there are some absolutes that we will never back away from: Provide the absolute best service, selection, and quality. Never steal from us or lie to us. Always make the customer happy. The day we think we've made it is the first day leading to our demise. Never stop 'running in a panic' to find ways to be better."

Employees were encouraged to find a better way, to do what it took to be better for our customers, then let us know what they did because we might want to do the same thing everywhere. Nobody was penalized for being creative with a customer as long as they intended to make that customer happy and they didn't violate one of the few rules listed above. This worked, and our business grew quickly. Those in leadership at that company talked continuously about—then set an example of—never removing our focus from the horizon and from wondering how we could improve ourselves or our efforts day by day. Those who failed to grasp the concept fell by the wayside and eventually ended up working somewhere else. The company expanded and grew exponentially over the years and remains a force today because the values are still there.

All organizations need to plan for their leaders of the future. Along with everything else that changes, they must have a pool of up and coming new leadership to take over the reins as those currently in place move on. I've heard it said that "you can't move up until you have somebody to take your place." The organizational culture determines how successful they will be at developing this pool of new and growing leaders who will successfully orchestrate the organization's journey into the future. Based upon my observations for the past forty years or so, here is what I believe:

1. If there are no strong leaders in the organization today, there will never be any strong leaders (without major change). It takes one to know one or to grow one. Weak leadership at the top cannot tolerate strong leadership below because there will always be a conflict in points of view. There will be an unhealthy atmosphere of competition between them. Good leadership candidates will go somewhere else.

2. Strong leaders will encourage others to, in a constructive manner, challenge or question the direction the organization is taking and will encourage others to recommend changes. They will recognize and reward those who present relevant ideas and give them credit for their recommendations. This environment encourages those within the organization to begin, and continue, looking ahead and around them for growth and improvement opportunities.

3. Strong leaders are risk-takers and are not afraid to try something new. They realize that not every new step will result in success. They encourage those around them to do the same by recognizing their efforts and by not penalizing mistakes made for the right reasons.

4. Strong leaders are not intimidated or threatened by their subordinates' successes. They applaud these successes publicly and reward those who are stepping up. They realize that their success is a result of the success of each member of the organization and that they cannot fight the fight alone. By encouraging subordinates to focus on the future and on improvements, they help them learn this process and it becomes a part of the culture of the organization.

5. Strong leaders search for and identify those within the organization who are exhibiting these characteristics and interests, and they find ways to place them in positions for

growth and development. By exposing them to new and growing challenges, these people develop their leadership skills instead of stagnating.

6. Strong leaders communicate often and loudly, organization-wide, about the organization's mission, vision, and values, and about the importance of leadership and excellence. There is no doubt in the mind of any member of the organization about what is important here and how we are doing.

7. Strong leaders expect excellence and the very best effort from every person, including themselves, every day. They cannot accept less. They also recognize the difference between effort and results and realize that results may not be there yet but will usually come in time. They recognize and reward the effort as well as the results. They make this part of the organizational culture too.

8. Strong leaders are decision makers. They solicit input and information then make a decision and take the credit or blame for their decision. They are willing to admit mistakes and take blame if necessary but set the example of leveraging the failures into successes next time. They expect and allow those around them to do the same.

9. Strong leaders attract and grow more strong leaders.

10. Without "succession planning" there will be no pool of leadership talent available for the future. The organization will be forced to settle for less or to go outside to find leadership, both of which are signs of impending demise and failure.

11. Future leaders should come from within the organization since this is the only way to ensure that they truly

understand the mission, vision, values, and culture. It also allows them to truly develop, exhibit, and demonstrate those attributes to the satisfaction of current leadership. Upon their promotion, they can hit the ground running without a learning curve relative to how our organization operates or what is expected.

Every organization goes through stages over time. In the beginning, somebody had a good idea and started it, brought in people to be a part of it, and put their time, talent, and effort into growing it into a success. Every organization is part of society and competes for its place in the pecking order with every other similar organization that surrounds it. Only by continual self-evaluation, improvement, and adjustment can an organization continue to be relevant and survive in the marketplace. Planning and preparing for the future is a critical part of the survival of any group because as those who are here today move up and move on they must be replaced by others who are as good, or better, than they were. This only occurs if there is a process in place to identify, groom, and develop these replacements.

A culture that encourages everyone to look for ways to grow and improve and that encourages people to recognize and develop leadership skills puts that organization in the best strategic position to survive long into the future. Organizations that experience some success then stop developing and improving will see that success slowly fade away and be replaced by those who seek to improve every day.

14
LEARNING TO APPRECIATE COMPLAINTS AND SUGGESTIONS

"About the only certainty, other than uncertainty, in fly fishing, is that a fly won't catch fish if it stays in its box."
–Arnold Gingrich

I RECEIVED AN EMAIL about a subordinate that began with a statement similar to, "Regarding the behavior of . . ." Now, I'm proud of every person who works with me, so my first response was a tightening in my chest and the beginnings of an angry reaction, because to me, the word "behavior" when applied to adults is condescending. Children behave or misbehave. Adults take action. Immediately, I started thinking, *Why didn't you just say regarding the actions of . . . instead of behavior?* As a human being, I instinctively react in a defensive way when I sense a complaint coming and was already building my defense based upon how the complaint was phrased. I was developing my response to let the sender of the email know that they were out of line addressing my subordinates in that unprofessional manner. I hadn't read the whole email yet, and I was discounting whatever the actual issue was going to be before I even knew what it was.

At an early age, we all learn defense mechanisms that allow us to deflect or redirect criticism, to blame somebody else, some circumstance, the originator of the criticism, our parents, ignore the criticism, or to, in some way, avoid having to address it directly. We do this because criticism is most often followed by something bad, such as discipline, loss of privileges, embarrassment, damage to our fragile ego, or loss of status. The ability to avoid taking responsibility for our actions has become an art form in our society. If we can build a proper defense at the first hint of criticism, maybe we can avoid it all together.

Here's the problem: Organizationally, if we truly strive to become excellent, it requires hearing from those we serve. Without feedback, our only measuring tool is our own perception, which is a woefully inadequate and inaccurate device. We must learn to appreciate the complaints, as well as the compliments, and to train ourselves to be totally objective as we investigate them.

As we will see, complaints, as well as compliments, suggestions, recommendations, and other feedback are really very valuable. They provide us opportunities to measure our performance and to be better than we would have been able to be without them. In fact, while compliments are nice to hear, and they are a means of confirmation that we are doing some things right, they don't really provide the opportunity for improvement that complaints provide. Therefore, it seems fair to say, complaints are actually more of a blessing than compliments.

To oversimplify what I mean, I'll use the example of registered mail with a return receipt. Frequently, we all send mail to destinations all over. We address the envelope, put a stamp on it, throw it into a mailbox, and forget about it, assuming it got to its destination. Most mail isn't so important, so we aren't too concerned that it might have failed to arrive. We know that our creditors will inform us if the payment doesn't get there, and, somewhere down the line, we'll notice that our magazine subscription never got renewed because the magazines stop arriving. Every once in a while though, we mail something important that absolutely must arrive at its destination, so we register it and ask for a return receipt signed by the recipient. This allows us to be certain that our message or product was received. In this case, we are sending out a message or product or something by mail and asking for feedback confirming the success of our effort to deliver this item.

The feedback we receive about the delivery of the mail allows us to be certain we were successful in our effort. In a way, this feedback is similar to a compliment. It says, "Thank you for satisfactorily completing this task in the expected manner." To carry this analysis a little further, what if the mail didn't arrive? We find this out quickly. We now have the equivalent of a complaint. We learn that we have not completed the intended task in the expected manner. Because we have been made aware of this, we now realize that we need to take corrective action. The receiver of the mail appreciates the fact that we took steps to monitor the results of our effort and that we remedied the situation quickly when the results were unsatisfactory.

Their satisfaction level remains higher than it would have been if we had not identified and fixed the problem. To take it another step, they tell those people around them that we are good guys because even though there was a problem with our service, we took an interest and jumped on it, resolving it to their satisfaction. Our reputation improves, and we improve our relationship with our customer base. Had we ignored them, or remained unaware of the problem, they would tell those same people about that too.

I'll relate one more illustration about how a complaint was a good thing, then move along with this discussion. In the late 1970s, I was the general store manager for a fashion clothing store in Southern California. A very angry woman came to the store office wanting to complain to the store manager, me. She was red in the face and very upset. I could also see that she was a person of influence, used to getting her way. My first reaction was, "Oh, oh. How am I going to get out of this one without getting in trouble?"

The woman explained that her daughter was getting married in a couple of days and that she had placed a mother of the bride dress on layaway with our store at some time in the past. The dress was to have been altered and was to be ready to pick up today. Now, we couldn't find her dress. So, what did I know at this point? The only important thing I needed to know was that we, or by default, I, messed this one up and it didn't appear there was any excuse whatsoever, nor did it matter to her if there was. The other thing I knew is that this lady was going to be at her daughter's wedding with many of our current and future customers and this topic was going to be right there at the top of the discussion list. I also knew we had made this event, which was already very stressful for a mother, even more stressful for this woman. To get to the point, I immediately admitted our guilt, had somebody take her around the store, find another dress she liked, alter it while she waited, refunded all of her money, and sent her a very large bouquet of flowers to the wedding from the store.

As a result of my actions with this customer, I made a friend for life, which was actually better than the result I was hoping to achieve. My point here is, without her complaint, as embarrassing as it was, I would never have had the opportunity to see and remedy a potential flaw in our system or to take the steps to satisfy her. Those actions saved a customer, hopefully earned us some new ones, and allowed us to prevent the same mistake from happening again to somebody else. The complaint turned out to be a gift. It allowed us to get better.

In everything we do, whether working with customers or internally with our associates and subordinates, it is absolutely essential that we continually self-examine the results of our efforts if we hope to improve. We can only see and understand so much from our side of the table, so it then becomes necessary to listen to the recipients who are on the receiving end. I'm not saying that we have to always agree with every input we receive, but I am saying that we must welcome every input because this gives us the chance to see things from a different perspective.

The idea that we have to allow others the opportunity to be right applies here. Any time a criticism is received, you must be able to say, as your first response, "Maybe they are right." Instinctively, we want to immediately take the position that they must be wrong, which eliminates any opportunity for us to improve, to actually receive the inherent benefit that comes with truly analyzing the disagreement.

While addressing complaints and complainers is unpleasant and often painful, it is part of being a leader. By meeting face to face with the person who disagrees, several benefits occur. It provides an opportunity to let them explain, in detail, their complaint, person to person. This eliminates any misunderstanding of the actual issues involved. It also provides an opportunity to ask one of the most important questions, "What did you expect would happen?" All of those we serve have an expectation of the level of service they will be provided. Usually, this expectation is reasonable but not every time. If we fell short of the reasonable expectation, we need to know that. If their expectation is unreasonable, we have an opportunity to recognize that as well. We can help them understand what is reasonable and why.

Remember, the person who is complaining is going to leave this meeting and discuss the results with other people who are also our customers or coworkers. Their conversation will generate far-reaching repercussions. This meeting allows us to review our actions in the light of the expectations of those we serve, as well as the expectations themselves, and provides a starting point for further investigation, if necessary. Meanwhile, two things must happen as a result of our receiving a complaint. First, we must thank the complainer for providing us this opportunity to review our processes and services. Second, in the end, regardless of whether we decide we have an opportunity to improve here or not, we must follow up with the complainer and explain the results.

Usually, the follow-up conversation with the person filing

the complaint follows the pattern of "Thank you so much for your input and for providing us this opportunity to check up on how we are doing. As a result of our investigation, the following actions were taken." It may turn out that the actions are "as we discussed earlier, our goal is to ____ and it appears we met that goal in this situation, so we did not take corrective action." What may have happened though is that this "complainer" may have actually just done us a favor and pointed out a way for us to improve, in which case it is imperative that we thank them for their input and let them know how we will be incorporating their idea into our way of operating in the future. Either response must also include a statement that we appreciate their input and we encourage further suggestions as they arise in the future.

When the complaint or suggestion is pointed at a subordinate or other associate, we, as effective leaders, need to help them develop the same response. As painful as complaints can be, they too need to understand that all successful people and organizations are either getting better or declining, but we can't get better unless we understand those opportunities for improvement. By helping them develop their response to complaints or suggestions, we assure them that they will be part of that process. It is also important that subordinates understand that complaints will not be viewed as merely an opportunity to hand out discipline but that they will actually be viewed as opportunities for all of us to grow. Of course, discipline or corrective action does apply when it turns out the complaint is the result of some intentional lack of follow-through or other incorrect action by an employee that warrants correction. While unpleasant, this too is a part of growth and is good for the overall organization since we, again, have an opportunity to improve.

Customers, subordinates, coworkers, and others who are influenced by our actions often have opinions, ideas, suggestions, corrections, or complaints about what we do. Only when we welcome this input and make a truly honest effort to identify those ideas that will help us improve and then incorporate them into what we do will we continue to get better. We must realize that these are the people who have the most important opinion regarding the results and success of our efforts. Our own opinion is woefully shortsighted and biased. Ego, personal insecurity, or personal pride have no place in leadership and will only prevent us from accomplishing our purposes in an excellent manner.

15
CONFLICT RESOLUTION, A CRITICAL SKILL

"Be patient and calm, for no one can catch fish in anger."
–Herbert Hoover

WE ALL LIKE THE image of the fearless leader, sword raised, up front, leading the charge toward the enemy. As we've discussed, excellent leaders are heard and seen by those they lead. They talk a lot about the mission, vision, and values and what they mean, how they relate to each member of the organization, how the organization is doing toward accomplishing them, what the future plans are, who is doing a great job, and all the other topics involved in keeping a team on track and motivated every day.

We also know that any time a team of people work together, or even spend time together, conflict occurs. Not everybody will like everybody else, nor will everybody agree with everything that is going on. Conflict can be internal, within the work group, or external with those the organization seeks to serve, with competitors, or the community in general. How the leader handles this conflict will have as equal an effect on the success of the organization as the efforts they put into those actions described in the opening paragraph.

Another way to look at this is to imagine a garden patch. The gardener tills the soil, removes the weeds, fertilizes, plants the crop, waters, and waits for the plants to come to maturity for the harvest. The plants have one job—to grow, be healthy, take in nutrients, water, and sunshine, and yield an excellent product. Sometime along the way, a weed is going to appear, at least in my gardens they do. Now, the gardener has a decision to make: Should they put in the effort to see the weed, identify it as a weed, and remove it? Or, since it's only one small weed, should they just ignore it rather than go through the bother of having to go out there and pull it out?

Certainly, one little weed will not affect the crop or the rest of the garden. In time, the little weed will grow and grow and will soon produce another little weed. Now, there is one big weed and a new little weed. It still has no measurable effect on the garden. Then the larger weed will sprout another little weed, and the new little weed will grow and send out new shoots and new little weeds of its own. Eventually, the weeds will begin using nutrients from the same soil that the crop is trying to use. At first, it will only affect a plant or two that are right where the weeds are. In my garden, there is never only one weed though. Eventually, another and another little weed will show up in other parts of the garden and will begin the same process as the first weed.

Now, each weed has a very small effect on the productivity of the garden, but, if left to grow and mature, this effect increases to the point where eventually it is increasing exponentially and, in the extreme case, the garden becomes choked out and the crops disappear among the weeds. One little weed at a time is easy to remove. Removing a garden full of weeds, left to grow uncontrolled, is an overwhelming task.

I think you can see where I'm going here. Conflicts within organizations are inevitable. People become angry, irritated, impatient, and frustrated with their coworkers and with the leadership. Customers become offended, and community members sometimes disagree with us. People talk about how they feel. That's human nature. We all want those around us to share our feelings, good or bad, so we spread them around.

In a work group, negative feelings become the weeds that grow, bloom, and spread more weeds until the dissatisfaction or unhappiness drowns out the positive efforts of others around them who are trying to stay on task. It is a proven fact that one unhappy, dissatisfied employee causes all of those in their group to feel some level of unhappiness and dissatisfaction as well, even if it's just because they have to work near that person. Conflict and dissatisfaction among people who are assigned to work together as team members breaks down their ability to cooperate and combine efforts toward a common goal. If people are unhappy with something in their personal situation, it will prevent them from being able to focus on the other tasks at hand.

Unhappy clients communicate with other potential clients as well, especially considering the prevalence and broad reach of social media. Their unhappiness will be spread around, person to person, until it reaches a level where it threatens our ability to grow or retain our market share and profitability.

Leadership absolutely must be sensitive to the flow around them, and they must notice and identify unhappiness or conflict. As humans, we all just want people to get over themselves and move on. We hate to invade others' space and personal business. We all know everybody has an occasional bad day and that most of the time people just work it out and move on. As leaders, we want everybody to do that every time there's a problem. True leaders recognize that isn't realistic and that there will be times they need to intervene. Since becoming involved in the problems or unhappiness of others is really unpleasant and often involves expending quite a bit of personal effort and energy, most leaders choose to wait as long as they can to get involved, on the chance that the issues will just work themselves out and go away. That choice is often a critical failure to lead.

I don't expect to get involved in every problem that comes up. Nobody wants to be micromanaged or confronted about all the little things that are happening in their life. There is a place where wisdom, experience, and common sense will tell the astute leader that something is going on, it's not going away, and it is headed toward the point where it will affect the others in the group or the organization as a whole. Immediately upon identifying these issues is the time to address them. Just as the gardener could have saved a big future problem by pulling the little weeds as soon as they were noticed, the excellent leader recognizes the fact that little problems are much easier to solve than big problems and that little problems, left unresolved, always grow into really big problems. If somebody isn't comfortable or willing to address and resolve conflicts when they show up, then they should never be in charge. Their effectiveness will diminish over time until they are drowned out by the unrest around them.

There is no magic formula to apply to conflict. Each will have its own personality requiring a unique application of wisdom on the part of the leader. The key is to sit down with the involved parties, individually at first, and get things out on the table. A good opening line is "I'm picking up a feeling that you aren't happy. Tell me what is going on." Of course, the most likely response will be, "I'm fine, it's okay." Here is where the unpleasant part starts. The conversation needs to continue until the issue is identified because nothing can be addressed until it is identified. This is the most critical step because, usually, after people tell you what the problem is, they are willing to work with you to solve it. People are often unhappy with the actions, statements, or perceived intentions of the organization or individual leaders within the organization. Sometimes, a new policy or rule is implemented and, absent a clear understanding of what brought it about, people create their own opinion of why and it is often totally inaccurate. By being sensitive to and keying in on this dissatisfaction, you have the opportunity to identify then address and resolve these concerns directly. This likely involves some individual discussions and a follow-up unit or organization-wide meeting to clear up the situation.

Problems between two or more people frequently present an obvious solution if all participants are seated in a group and each is allowed and encouraged to speak their mind while each of the others listens and says nothing, until their turn to speak. After everybody has spoken, it often becomes clear that the whole issue is because of some misunderstanding that happened someplace back in the past. Somebody said or did something that somebody else misunderstood or misinterpreted. The second person was irritated or hurt by it but never said anything so the issue was never resolved. The feelings remained though. Over time, the first person recognizes that the second person doesn't like them so they mirror those feelings back. Eventually, the feelings will spread with the possibility of involving all the other coworkers who may take sides with one participant or another. On the other hand, if the original two people are allowed to express their concerns to each other in a calm manner, they usually realize that their issue was based on a simple misunderstanding and there's no basis for it. They get over it and move on.

As previously stated, I'm not going to try to suggest a solution to every situation that could occur. I am going to emphasize a few common observations though. Usually, conflict will not go away by itself. Conflict spreads and grows, affecting more and more people until it is resolved. New conflict that has not spread and grown is much easier to deal with and resolve than old conflict that has affected many people. People expect and appreciate it when the leader assertively addresses conflict, and they are disappointed and lose respect when they don't. An effective leader must be willing to tackle conflict quickly and directly if the efforts of the entire work group are to be kept focused on the mission of the organization.

Many people in leadership positions hesitate to become involved in conflict resolution, which is a critical error on their part. If the feelings of dissatisfaction being exhibited by the subordinate involve the actions of the leader, they need to be addressed as well. Examine yourself from an unbiased position and give the other person the opportunity to be right before you decide they are wrong. If that person has a valid concern, admit it and make the changes to resolve it. It must be clear that the dysfunctional situation must be and will be resolved and that it cannot continue. The end of the conversation must always include a clear definition of the problem, the required solution, and the understanding on the part of those who need to make changes that the "ball is in your court, and it's up to you to show me what you can do" relative to resolving the situation. A person who is repeatedly the source of unrest may have to be removed from the group if that's what it takes to return harmony to the overall organization.

One last observation: Only when the efforts to address the problems are applied in a positive, creative manner will they be effective. If the leader addresses the participants in a way that appears to be insulting, scolding, demeaning, or some other type of personal attack, the problem will likely magnify itself as soon as the meeting is over. The process must proceed in a positive, productive manner, but people must also understand that this is important and it must be put behind us so that we can refocus on the important tasks at hand. The issues must be addressed in a way that allows the team members to retain their personal dignity and feeling of self-worth.

In essence, the leader must convey the following: "You are an important member of this organization. I want you to continue to be a member of my team here, but I need your help in getting back on track. For that to happen, it's going to be necessary for you to ____" (clearly identify the changes necessary). People then need a deadline for the resolution of the issues or for the necessary changes to be completed. "I prefer to schedule a follow-up meeting fairly soon, at which point we will get together and touch base. I expect we will agree at that time that we have moved on beyond this problem or at least that we are well on our way."

Individual counseling or reprimands must be done privately. Whatever happens or is revealed in the process is confidential and nobody else's business. The person with the conflict must believe that the leader is trying to work with them and is "on their team." Often, they will not get the answer they wish for, but they must know that they were given a fair opportunity to speak their mind and address their concerns. The leader must make a clear decision and identify a course of action that must occur. It may be similar to "I know you will never be best friends with ___ and I don't expect you guys to go to lunch or socialize, but while you're working together I expect you to cooperate and keep your feelings under control."

It's not glamorous or enjoyable, but an excellent leader is required to be excellent in addressing and resolving conflict.

16

JUST BECAUSE YOU'RE TIRED, DOESN'T MEAN YOU'RE DONE

"If you've got short stubby fingers, and wear reading glasses, any relaxation you would normally derive from fly fishing is completely eliminated when you try to tie on a fly."
–Jack Ohman

THE STATEMENT "JUST BECAUSE you're tired doesn't mean you're done," although improper grammar, was a family saying when our daughters were at home. It served them and us well as a reminder that the work isn't finished until the job is done right. There was an old Chris LeDoux song in those days titled "Five Dollar Fine" that talked about a fine for whining. We sang it as a family whenever it came on the cassette player while we were traveling. Yes, cassette. I know, it dates me.

When I was young, my parents never gave me an allowance but allowed me to earn money by completing chores. My father left me a list: Clean the dog pen, cut and stack firewood, pull weeds, mow the lawn—whatever he picked for the job of the day. When my chores were completed to his satisfaction, I was often rewarded with some financial compensation. I recall discussing the fact that some of my friends received allowances that didn't have associated tasks attached to them. His answer shaped my view of things for the rest of my life: "Don't ever expect something for nothing. That's lazy." We, as a society, have tried so hard to avoid hurting our children's feelings that we have, in many cases, taught them to expect something for nothing. We've lost the idea that "an honest day's work deserves an honest day's pay."

Why is any of this worth mentioning? During my lifetime, society's expectations about the level of effort people should expend has changed. Just to make sure I'm not misunderstood here, I know a lot of people who work really hard at what they do, and I'm not making a blanket statement. Those people are special and a blessing to be around. What I see more of now than I did in the past is people and groups of people, employed by various organizations, who are primarily focused on the level of effort that will be required of them instead of on the task that they are assigned to complete.

Today, many people are so concerned about how hard they might have to work, how much time they might have to spend, how much detail might be expected of them, and so many other things related to expending the least amount of effort to get by, that they have totally lost sight of the reason they are putting in the effort in the first place. I'm sorry if I offend somebody, but I call this "lazy."

Organizations exist to provide products or services to customers. In previous discussions, we have established that customers, the beneficiaries of the products and services, have a reasonable expectation of quality. In fact, they reasonably expect value and their money's worth along with good quality. They don't expect mediocre, less than satisfactory products. We have also established that the leadership of any organization has to decide how excellent they want to be before there is any hope of finding improvement. Employers also have a right to the same expectations. They invest in employees and have a right to expect reasonable value and quality in return for the pay they invest. Each organization must answer the question, "What is reasonable?"

Every leader dreams of having a crew of all hard-working, conscientious employees who spare no effort to provide the best products and services. Every leader with any experience at all will tell you "dream on" when you hope for one of those. Every leader with a goal of providing excellence must learn how to bring out the best effort from every employee, associate, or crew member. What motivates people to put their heart and soul into their work?

Earlier, we discussed expectations. Once again, as in every case, this has to start with the company owner or the very top person on the organizational chart. Unless the very top person is leading the charge by setting, or at least, agreeing with the standards, no lower-level supervisor will be able to effectively improve the output and quality of the work produced by their unit. Those who don't like it will just complain up the chain of command, which will result in the statement "Stop, you're making the rest of us look bad" being sent to this ambitious guy. And once again, it's going to take a lot of work, every day, and generate a lot of frustration, but the results will make the effort worthwhile.

The focus of every member of the organization has to be on the mission, vision, and values of the organization. People need to know, understand, and buy into why this organization exists and what the organizational expectation is. It must be written, spoken, and modeled daily by all those in leadership roles. A second part of the equation is that people must understand why they personally should even care to live up to the mission, vision, and values. Why does it make a difference and why should I do that has to be answered in each person's mind. Obviously, step one is to make it clear, in the performance expectations, what must be fulfilled to keep the job. The expectation must focus on who we are and how we operate and the mindset or culture of our organization as reflected in our work ethic. That's the least effective of the steps, though because, as we discussed in the opening paragraphs, many people know exactly where the minimum performance line is and will expend great effort not to put in any more effort than that. Somebody is always testing the boundary to see if it moved since last time they tested it. Everybody else watches to see the result.

We already established that the hiring process is the first place where this effort gets a boost. Those responsible for hiring must have a clear picture of this in their minds. They have to explore this thing called "work ethic" with each job candidate and find out how that person looks at working within an organization, our organization. Once again, we need people who are focused on the result of the effort—producing great products and services that they can take pride in, not so much on the process. We have to find answers to the questions, "Do they take pride in providing quality products and services? Do they have an opinion about what makes our organization special? Why do they want to join us? What do they want to contribute to our organization?"

If the job candidate can provide some answers to those questions then we see that they at least have the ability to focus on what we believe is important. On the other hand, if they don't really know the answers and their conversation focuses on pay, hours, benefits, time off, and how bad their last boss was and what a conspiracy there was at that place to get rid of them, then we can get a pretty good idea of where their focus will be if they join our organization.

In an earlier chapter, we discussed Maslow's hierarchy of needs. People must believe that their basic needs are being covered before they can focus on higher-level topics. Employees must feel that they are appreciated, have a secure job, and that they are being fairly compensated in terms of pay, benefits, and working conditions before we can ever expect them to move their focus off of those things to higher-level pursuits. This will be the topic of another chapter, but leadership must also continually communicate why this organization and the products and services it provides are great, the greatest. Of course, if the leadership can't do this in a way that people understand and believe in, they will have no credibility and the leadership itself will be a failure.

Most people want to be part of something great. When the home team is winning, the stands at the ballpark are full; vice versa when they are having a losing season. We have to help people understand and believe that they are members of a winning team. This is so important because winners then want to act like winners. A key thing here though is that if the organization isn't really excellent at this point, don't try to convince the members that it is. They know the truth. Change the focus to "we are all part of a great team that is rebuilding," and focus frequently on the progress that is being made toward being the winning team. People will still feel good about being part of something good.

In the early 1980s, I worked for a company where the president, during his presentations to employees, the media, and public, frequently said, "We manage by contest, and any time we find something we need to improve we make a contest out of it." He was right, and the contests involved all members of the organization, not just sales or the high-visibility groups. They were a lot of fun for everyone. We had contests for everything: cleanest store, highest sales increase, best improvement in energy expense, and on and on; and they had a huge impact on the way problems got ironed out. People were motivated to do their best because pride was at stake. Contests have to be done in the right spirit. They have to be a positive thing, well promoted, and set up fairly. The "prize" needs to be meaningful. As I said earlier, people like to be winners, on a winning team. The caveat of this is that the contest must not divide groups or generate discord between work groups. The result must build on the greatness of the organization as a whole.

I cannot emphasize enough the importance of recognizing those people and groups who are doing well. You will get tired of me talking about this, but it has to be ongoing and frequent. Every member of the organization must believe that hard work, quality work is important here and that, when they do this kind of work, they will be appreciated and recognized. For instance, some places are able to provide financial rewards for quality performance. I'm 100 percent in favor of incentive bonuses when they are designed to enhance the greater good of the organization. Sales commissions and piece work pay are also great motivators for people to work hard because they receive personal benefit for doing so. Profit-sharing programs, shares of company stock—any time people can be made partners who participate in and benefit from the success of the organization—is a good thing as well.

Meanwhile, many organizations can't provide financial rewards, and that is when the recognition and appreciation from leadership pays such big dividends. Most people appreciate a compliment and the recognition that they did something well. At the most rudimentary level, people work for money, but their approach to the job is a result of how they feel about the job and about themselves when they are doing the job.

On the negative side, and we discussed this in a previous chapter but I'm going to repeat it, there will always be people who do not respond to anything and are going to focus on getting by with the minimum effort. Those people need to be identified early on, counseled, and made to understand that the expectations of the organization are not negotiable. They also must understand clearly that "the ball is in their court" and that they have the opportunity to show the leadership that they can live up to the level of performance around them.

Part of the counseling for a poor performer must include a clear statement that mediocre work cannot be accepted here and that they are in control of whether they continue to be employed here or not. This is their opportunity to show us what their choice is going to be. As frustrating and difficult as it is, people who do not respond must be removed from the organization, because, if allowed to continue, their level of effort will become considered an acceptable level by virtue of the fact that it has been accepted over a period of time. In my experience, in an organization with active and effective leadership, this will involve very few employees, but these employees will have a major effect on everybody around them if left to continue in their ways. Sometimes, it doesn't work though, then the hard choice becomes the right one. This is not the right fit for them, and they need to go someplace else where they will fit in.

Hard work and good work are less common concepts than maybe they were in years past. They are certainly not lost concepts and are most certainly attainable in any organization but only if the leadership makes the idea that excellence and pride in who we are and what we do are a part of the organizational culture. Motivating people to bring their best effort is a critical function of any person in a position of leadership.

17
WHAT IS THE REAL MISSION?

"Fishing is much more than fish . . . It is the great occasion when we may return to the fine simplicity of our forefathers."
–Herbert Hoover

"Mission Statement":
   A mission statement is a statement of the purpose of a <u>company,</u> <u>organization,</u> *or* <u>person</u>; *its reason for existing.*
   — My own definition

We all have a mission both individually and collectively as groups or organizations. The mission directs and focuses our efforts and thoughts. It is the X that we are headed toward on the map and the destination in the "go-to" box on our internal GPS. When we get up in the morning, our subconscious mind resets itself for the day and brings up the picture of "what I want to accomplish today." Then, our mission is reset and we focus on the objective that has become center-screen for today, whatever that is. We have the ability to decide what will be important today and thereby focus our efforts on that subject.

We all spend our time trying to do something. If we are hungry, our mission is to find something to eat. If we are cold, it is to get warm and maybe to stay warm. Maybe we are trying to save enough money or get a good enough credit rating to buy a new car, or boat, or house. Possibly, it's to get the promotion we want, or the new job, or a spouse. We focus a lot of time, thought, and energy on our personal "core" mission. There are levels of missions as well. We have personal missions, family missions, missions we define for our children, organizational missions, unit or group missions within the organization, and the list goes on and on.

I'm going to talk about organizational missions. As the definition at the beginning of this chapter says, the mission "*is a statement of the purpose of a company, organization, or person; its reason for existing.*" As such, it seems to me that the mission must be very carefully defined for each organization. Without a clear, well-defined mission, it's hard for anybody to know what we are trying to do. In the absence of good information, people make up their own to fill in the blanks. That means, in the absence of a clearly defined mission, people just come up with their own definition of the mission. Clearly, that leads to divergent, fragmented effort with no specific focus.

As you can see, I'm beginning to draw a picture here. On one side of the page, we have a bunch of stick figures representing people involved in the organization. Each of these figures has an arrow pointing to their idea of the organizational mission. The arrow represents the effort they expend while involved in the activities of the organization—working, volunteering, whatever. Now, we have two pictures. One has a circle titled "clearly defined mission" on the other side of the page. Notice how all the arrows point directly toward that circle. The other page has no clearly defined mission. The arrows point randomly around the page toward each person's idea of what the mission should be.

There's always a mission. The guy who started the organization had something in mind in the beginning. The question is, "Does everybody here know what that mission is?" If we want people to focus their effort, we have to tell them where we are going. That's the easy part, and it's where most organizations stop. Somebody or some group sits down and develops a mission statement that says something like, "Our mission is to (insert mission of choice)." Then they print it on papers that get hung all over the place, on the entry door, over the urinal, on the microwave, at the top of the website, on the front of the brochure, on the back of the cars, wherever. Mission accomplished, now let's go to lunch.

I mean that last sentence seriously. This is the point where most organizations fail. They don't really direct everybody's focus toward the mission. They believe that "just because we told people about what we think the mission should be, everybody will get on board and focus all of their effort on accomplishing it. Our job is done here." Wrong answer. Now, the real work begins.

As we discussed at the beginning, we each have levels of missions that focus our effort. The most important mission to me right now may not be the organizational mission statement I read on the front door awhile back. I may not even remember what that said. As a typical participant in an organization, I may not even care what that said because I just came here for the paycheck so I can buy the new boat that is on my *personal* mission statement. Part of the process of developing the organizational mission is to make it something people can identify with, that they have a reason to believe in.

If the organization is to succeed, the mission must also become the primary focus of each member of that organization, at least while they are involved in organizational activities. The very top executive officer of the organization carries primary responsibility for this. That person must truly be able to visualize the mission, then they must live the mission, communicate the mission, and set the example to everyone else of what the mission looks like in action. Every other leader below that level must then take that and model it themselves. The mission must be talked about regularly throughout the organization until there is no doubt what it is, what it looks like, and what it means. Even the person who cleans the desks at night has to understand the mission.

The mission has to be divided into sub-missions, if you will, that define the contribution each unit or person makes to achieving the overall organizational mission. Each person has to know how we are doing toward accomplishing the mission at all times. Then each person has to know why we should want to accomplish this mission in the first place, why it is a good thing. This is a big deal. People not only need to understand the mission, but they need to know why it is something good for them to be a part of. If, by succeeding at this mission the company will become more profitable, which means I get to continue in my job or get better paychecks, that is good. If it means we are bringing about some social good that I and my community will benefit from, that is good. Whatever it is, they need to believe that the mission is good and worth accomplishing.

You can force people to work toward the mission, or you can help them want to accomplish the mission because they believe in it. It's pretty easy to figure out which works better. Somebody somewhere has to have their finger on the pulse. By spending time with the people who are part of the organization, it's pretty easy to read how they feel about the mission and the organization in general. The very top people in the management structure are that somebody.

We all get distracted and start looking around, so we need to be reminded to continue to focus our effort. Most organizations experience this from time to time. As we discussed earlier, a mission is defined and sent around then distractions immediately come along to change the focus of those people who are trying to get the job done. Let's just use a law enforcement organization as an example. Their published mission goes something like, "Making Our Community Safer." The people who work there like that and agree with the mission.

Here's what happens though. Being in law enforcement, they naturally tend to focus on the negative. There's a guy (internal affairs) who is there solely to investigate what people did wrong. They also have an elaborate system of collecting, investigating, and filing personnel complaints about what went wrong. There is a carefully designed matrix of discipline options to apply to the complaints and a very thick policy and procedure manual to define how to do everything and to make sure there is a clear rule to put on the personnel complaint form. In the current state of our society, the agency, and others like it, spend a tremendous amount of effort trying not to do something wrong because then somebody might sue them or they might get negative press in the media. That looks bad and might get the top management criticized. Now, they don't want to violate anybody's rights and don't want to hurt anybody. They catalog and file every use of force, employee-involved vehicle accident, the number of complaints each employee has received, anybody who becomes involved in a vehicle pursuit, etc. It might be easy to conclude that the most important thing here is to stay out of trouble. Then sometime during the year, the organization spends too much money and has to start cutting back to prevent overrunning the budget. Overtime gets reduced, and people receive the message and do more with less.

Now, the most important thing might be not spending money. Someplace in the organization is a crabby administrator who irritates the work group they are associated with, and those people put in extra effort to avoid him. Then a new computer system comes along that changes the way everybody does business. Everybody becomes involved in either trying to learn how to use it or hoping it crashes and burns so they don't have to use it. Is anybody even thinking about making the community safer? Probably not. What happened here is that some people are focused on the mission of staying out of trouble, others are focused on not spending money, while some are focused on avoiding the administrator or mastering the new computer system. We have a multitude of missions.

I'm not picking on this particular industry. I just happen to have some experience in it. This process happens everywhere. A manufacturing company wants to make the best product in the world but falls into the trap of not wanting to offend the union, so they start compromising their expectations or how they interface with employees. The employees start talking about how bad the management treats them. The policy manual starts getting thicker and thicker so they can define every infraction an employee might commit. They get off course.

Then in the case of sales organizations, they want to provide the best selection and service and have the most satisfied customers but, as they pressure the employees to produce more and more, those employees start putting together deals that get sales even if it's not in the customers' best interests. The short-term goal gets met, but the long-term mission is sacrificed. The real mission becomes to maximize sales at all costs. The whole financial crisis of the past years happened as a result of people losing focus of the overall mission of organizations and shifting to ways to maximize their short-term benefit, at the expense of the whole world this time. Organizations actually make it difficult for their members to accomplish the mission by placing multiple roadblocks and obstacles in the way. They cause employees to have to choose between the stated mission and the informal mission that is being practiced around them. The informal one always wins.

As a result of all of the distractions, management becomes involved in putting out the "daily fires" and finds themselves immersed in multiple projects and crises as well. Somebody has to be the watchdog who realizes what is happening and continually refocuses the efforts of the group. In spite of all the distraction, the overall focus has to be on the organizational mission. There will always be distractions. These become "sub-missions" that must be resolved or accomplished, but the efforts of the people involved in the organization have to be brought back to center every time and each of these sub-missions must point to, support, and contribute to the overall organizational mission.

Another piece of this, which I've touched on, is that people need to know why they should be interested in accomplishing the organizational mission in the first place. They also need to know how we, as an organization, are doing. It is important that along with communicating the mission, management also communicates why this is a good mission. If it means our community will be better because of us, or our company will continue to grow, thereby enabling it to continue employing all of us, or we will all get sales bonuses, or whatever other reason, this has to be communicated and it has to be personalized for each employee. People need to understand their part and why they are important as well as why it's important, and a good thing, to pursue the stated mission. It is equally important to provide periodic updates on how the organization is doing at accomplishing the mission.

Somebody needs to collect information about how the mission is being met and to communicate it to everybody who is involved. If it's good news, that's great. If it's not so good, they need to know that too and to be involved in making it better. When those involved in leadership know things aren't going so well but don't tell anybody, except for sending out the new directives to sell more, spend less, etc., people don't accept those directives well. When everybody is aware and involved, a team identity is formed and it becomes "we" who are doing our best to make this better and people accept the "directives" because they understand and agree with the reasons for them. My point is, the mission has to be a part of daily focus and discussion, and everybody must identify with it. Somebody needs to take the responsibility to make this happen, and they need to have the "big picture" view organizationally to recognize when distractions are changing the focus.

We each have missions. We have personal, family, and organizational missions. Missions are the most powerful motivational tool in society. To accomplish the mission of the organization to which we belong, we have to clearly understand that mission and our role in achieving it. Our effort must be focused then refocused on the mission, and we have to continually monitor how we are doing on our path toward it.

Organizationally, every member must have the same overall mission and must understand their role. Every member must believe in the mission and must agree that accomplishing it is a desirable thing not only for the organization but for them personally. The primary force responsible for this is the very top executive person at that organization. It must start at the top. It requires unwavering focus and energy at every level. Those in control of the organization must guard that mission and take responsibility for the direction and focus of that organization every day.

18
GIVE PEOPLE A REASON TO BE EXCITED

"If people concentrated on the really important things in life, there'd be a shortage of fishing poles."
–Doug Larson

LET'S EXPAND ON THE previous chapter where we discussed missions and how they should be developed in such a way that people believe they are worthwhile to pursue. Every business, every organization that provides any sort of product or service has a mission or goal to provide good customer service or to do excellent work or to produce excellent products. Organizational administrators have, *ad nauseam*, told their employees that they must give great service or produce great products. They spend millions on advertising campaigns trying to convince the marketplace that theirs is the best. They make up catchy mottos to hang on the walls or put at the bottom of the letterhead or web page, and they hire quality control folks to report back to management about quality stuff. Sometimes they get it right but oftentimes they don't.

I truly believe organizations that really provide excellent products and services don't need to tell the market about it. After a while, the marketplace will be telling them how much they like their work. If you have to work to convince people that your products or services are good then there's a good chance they aren't really that great. Excellent work done consistently over time produces an excellent reputation which then spreads throughout the marketplace. Word of mouth becomes the best advertising because it is based upon personal experience not some lofty claim made by the organization. People are looking far and wide for excellence and are excited when they find it. They can't wait to spread the good news. I believe there is a place for advertising, of course, but you can't convince people you are excellent; you have to show them and give them a reason to be excited. Remember the saying, "Actions speak louder than words"? It is absolutely true. It's also true that it's impossible to convince those you serve that you are excellent unless you, and those associated with you, believe it first.

In the 1970s and early 1980s, I worked for Nordstrom. They spent significantly less than their competitors on advertising yet produced nearly double the sales per square foot of merchandising space than those same competitors. How did that work? Their mission was to provide the finest service, selection, and quality to every customer. Customers truly experienced excellent service, selection, and quality when they shopped at Nordstrom, so it became their first stop whenever they went shopping. People talked about it, and the word spread. The company didn't have to tell the marketplace because the marketplace already knew it; people had found out for themselves.

At Nordstrom, company leadership spent considerable effort ensuring that the people who were involved in the company knew why it was a great place and what made it that way. They talked about the communication they received from happy customers. They talked about how sales were going, the company's profitability, the upcoming expansion and the opportunities that growth would provide for everyone, about how great everybody who worked there was, how great and special the customers were, how we were doing compared to our competitors, why our products were the best available, and overall, again and again, about how critically important every single employee was to accomplishing the mission. These conversations happened somewhere around the company every single day. The employees knew why we were special and truly believed it. They showed that to every customer who walked through the door. They also understood that, if the standards ever slipped, customers would figure that out before the company did and spend money elsewhere. Each of us realized we had to be our best, every day, to keep it going.

No organization will ever be able to develop a reputation for excellence until the employees of that organization are given a reason to be proud and excited and to truly believe the organization is excellent. Leadership must create an environment and build a culture that allows and expects employees to be their very best. Leadership must "lead" the way by putting the environment in place that allows employees to produce excellent products and services. They must encourage employees to be participants, and they must treat their employees as valuable, essential members of the whole process. Leadership must show, by their actions and their service, that they are excited and proud to be a part of this organization and are willing to do what it takes to give their employees every tool, material, encouragement, and whatever else they need to be their best.

If employees have the materials and training they need and are in an environment where they believe they are appreciated and supported, not coddled by the way, they are more likely to give their best effort. Leadership must give employees a reason to be excited and to be proud of what they do and who they are. Employees need information too, so that they truly understand why their organization is great, why they themselves are great, and why their products or services are great. There is no such thing as giving employees too much of the right kind of information. They need to understand why it is good for them to be a part of this organization and why the organization is growing or improving or becoming better all the time. They also need to know why this organization is great for their customers or clients. They need to know why the products or services they offer, or produce, are the best available. When they understand, and believe, they will pass it on.

As for customers, they never see, or even recognize, top organizational leadership. The only people customers ever come in contact with are the first-line employees. It doesn't matter one bit to the customers what leadership believes because the people they see, hear from, and work with are those first-line employees. When those people are excited and proud to be a part of the organization, and are excited about and proud of the products they represent, the customers will know it and be excited too. It's so contagious that you can't stop it from spreading.

Likewise, it doesn't matter one bit what leadership thinks or wants. If the first-line employees don't believe the product or service is worth getting excited about then the customers will get that message too. Only excited, happy, proud employees produce and reproduce excellence. This will show up in their work product, their services, and their sales results, and it will spread to customers whenever they interact with them. Employees can only become excited and happy when they know why they should be, which only happens when leadership shares the information they need to truly understand it. Spread it around.

Again, it must start at the very top of the organization. Unless leadership steps up and sets the tone, by their example, and gives people a reason to be excited to be here, there will be no excellence. Leadership cannot convince the marketplace that some excellent state of being exists by any amount of advertising and promotion if it does not. Only true excellence will convince the market, and it will advertise itself.

19
NEVER MISTAKE EGOTISM FOR CONFIDENCE

"I prefer any kind of fishing to any kind of work."
–Ed Zern

*IF YOU HAVE **SELF-CONFIDENCE**, you behave confidently because you feel sure of your abilities or value*
  — Collins English Dictionary

Confidence is one of the necessary qualities of a successful leader. A successful leader must believe in themselves and their ability to understand and sort out the variables at hand; and, in the end, they must arrive at the best solution to the challenges in their path. They must believe in themselves and their ability enough to make timely decisions and to take positive action when it is needed. People expect those who take on leadership roles to be confident, comfortable with their role, and decisive. This confidence spreads throughout the work group and generates a sense of calm and well-being at all levels.

Unfortunately, confidence in leadership is not as common as it should be. The confidence I'm describing comes from a place of acceptance of oneself, "sure of one's value" paired with the belief that "I'm able and willing to do this job." This belief in one's ability comes from experience and the overcoming of many challenges on the path that leads up to this day and this challenge. This belief in one's ability must be tempered with humility because the true leader knows they are not an island, the only source of inspiration and creativity, but in fact they are, most importantly, the conduit through which the inspiration and creativity around them is funneled toward the end goal of overcoming the next challenge or developing the next great idea.

A truly confident leader must be sure of their own personal value; in other words, they must be okay with and believe in themselves first before they can allow others to become involved in, and possibly receive recognition for, the process. The truly self-confident, effective leader realizes the value of others and strives to involve all members of their team in the process as much as possible. They work to bring out, and incorporate, the best ideas and information from all involved during the day-to-day search for solutions. The confident leader is not afraid to ask, "What do you think?" A person must be okay with themselves before they can help others grow and succeed around them.

Additionally, a confident leader must be able to separate their personal sense of self-worth from the day-to-day give and take that is part of their organizational role. They must truly know that believing in others and allowing others to grow, bloom, and succeed is not a threat to their own personal success. In fact, they must be able to watch those they influence improve and succeed with a true sense of satisfaction and pride, even if those people take the spotlight away from time to time. A confident leader knows that the entire team plays a role in the successes and should share in the recognition for those successes as well. As I said earlier, true self-confidence and confident leadership require the leader to be okay with themselves and their own sense of self-worth first before they can be pleased with the success of those around them. These people understand that success means everybody in the work group grows and wins. "We" must be more important than "me."

In the end, they know that it's on them to choose the apparent best alternative and make the important decisions when they need to be made. Their self-confidence allows them to be comfortable in this role, and they feel good about their decisions because they are based upon experience and solid information gained from all available sources. In the event that the decision doesn't yield the desired result, they accept responsibility for the result rather than look for a way to pass on the blame.

A confident leader inspires their subordinates to develop their own confidence as well by allowing them to share in the development of solutions to the challenges of day-to-day operations. This confidence then leads to greater and greater achievements and success as the subordinates learn to believe in themselves and to reach for even greater successes without fear of reprisal, as is often the case of working with an egotistical leader. It's the ability to recruit those around them to share in the development of ideas and solutions along with the ability to, in the end, be decisive and choose the course of action that sets apart those leaders who would be truly labeled as confident.

Another type of leader, who often masquerades as confident, is the egotistical leader. As with the confident leader, this person is often decisive and is pushing forward through the daily challenges, but their source of motivation is diametrically opposed to that of the confident person.

Wikipedia describes it like this: ***"Egotism"***:

Egotism *is the drive to maintain and enhance favorable views of oneself, and generally features an inflated opinion of one's personal features and importance. The egotist has an overwhelming sense of the centrality of the 'Me', that is to say of their personal qualities. Egotism means placing oneself at the core of one's world with no concern for others, including those "loved" or considered as "close," in any other terms except those subjectively set by the egotist.*

Interestingly enough, those who operate from this position, while sometimes appearing confident, usually suffer from a serious lack of self-esteem and self-worth. They are not okay with themselves or their abilities, even though they may try to appear as if they are. They may be decisive but are also the proverbial "micromanagers," taking great pains to make sure that they are in control of everything that happens and that nobody departs from their plan. They don't involve others in the idea development or strategy portions of the job and do not solicit input from others in the work group. In fact, they resist and criticize ideas or suggestions from others. If they are criticized or questioned, they become angry. Their conversation often includes frequent references to the words "me" or "I" and generally does not include "we" or "us," at least when describing successes.

Furthermore, egotistical leaders tend to isolate themselves from their subordinates, only appearing when they have some pronouncement to make or to pass out orders. They rarely say thank you, or good job, or I knew you could do it, and they avoid passing on reports of their subordinates' good deeds and accomplishments to others in the organization.

The core problem is that these people operate from a position where their sense of self-worth is contingent upon receiving positive personal credit for the outcome of every challenge or project they or their work group faces, and they believe life is a contest every day with only one person, themselves, receiving the credit for those outcomes. If another person receives credit for a positive result, these people view it as threatening to their personal status in the eyes of those around them. They don't understand that it's okay for others to do well and that when everybody does well we are all better off every time. The creativity and good suggestions of subordinates are viewed as a threat because others may see them as the leader's failure to not think of the good idea first.

The leader suffering from low self-esteem is very much committed to making the rules and defining the process, leaving no room for personal creativity or questioning of the status quo by their subordinates. In this environment, creativity dies and the personal motivation of subordinates evaporates, causing successes and growth to eventually flatline. Subordinates merely follow the steps handed down to them, never considering the possibility that there may be a better way to do things. They have no respect for the leadership abilities of egotistical leaders and, as a result, they put little effort into working with them to improve anything. In fact, subordinates usually spend a lot of time complaining amongst themselves about such people.

We've discussed similar ideas in earlier chapters, but these concepts are so important so I felt that we should look at them again. Confidence in leadership is a required attribute. True confidence is contagious throughout the organization, and the successes experienced by all involved grow as a result of its presence. Excellence can only be achieved if each person involved in the organization develops an excellent attitude. Self-confidence that is strong enough to allow the leader to delight in and applaud the successes of their subordinates, combined with a true sense of humility at all levels of the organization, are foundational building blocks of excellence.

20
EMPATHY, BUILDING PARTNERSHIPS

"Fly-fishing is not about catching the fish. It is about enjoying the water, the breeze, the fish swimming all around. If you catch one, good. If you don't . . . that is even better. That means you come out and get to try it all over again."
–Clare Vanderpool

IN THE LAST CHAPTER, we addressed confidence as an essential quality found in excellent leaders. Building on that discussion, we find that empathy, the ability and desire to share the situation, feelings, and emotions of another person, is another quality found in all excellent leaders. In researching empathy, I found an interesting conclusion in *Wikipedia*:

In the 2009 book Wired to Care, *strategy consultant Dev Patnaik argues that a major flaw in contemporary business practice is a lack of empathy inside large corporations. He states that lacking any sense of empathy, people inside companies struggle to make intuitive decisions and often get fooled into believing they understand their business if they have quantitative research to rely upon. Patnaik claims that the real opportunity for companies doing business in the 21st Century is to create a widely held sense of empathy for customers, pointing to Nike, Harley-Davidson, and IBM as examples of "Open Empathy Organizations". Such institutions, he claims, see new opportunities more quickly than competitors, adapt to change more easily, and create workplaces that offer employees a greater sense of mission in their jobs. In studies by the Management Research Group, empathy was found to be the strongest predictor of ethical leadership behavior out of 22 competencies in its management model, and empathy was one of the three strongest predictors of senior executive effectiveness.*

In the beginning, we discussed how meeting peoples' needs is so important to the success of any group or entity. The people we are talking about here are fellow workers, employees, and customers, or those who receive or benefit from our services. People have levels of needs from the most basic (survival, food, and shelter)—to the highest (self-actualization), and they are unable to focus on the next level until they believe the lower-level needs are addressed. As an organization, it is important to have all participants focused on providing excellent, high-quality service and products, and the only way that happens is if the distractions are minimized and people are allowed to focus and perform at that level. Only when people have a true sense of security and well-being in their work situation can they focus all of their effort on providing excellent output.

On the customer side, they purchase or use the products or services provided to the degree that they believe they address the solution of some need. The role of leadership is to maintain the level of satisfaction and focus throughout the organization every day. It's a fact—people care about and respond positively to those who truly care about them.

Sympathy is often mistaken for empathy. Empathy is the ability to *understand* and *vicariously experience* the feelings of others, to place yourself in their position, while sympathy is *caring* for the feelings of others. There is a significant difference in the level of effort involved in these two concepts. We all agree that we should be concerned about others' feelings. In society, there are people everywhere wanting us to accept them or believe they and their cause are important. It's not hard to be sympathetic to the situations of others, but to actually experience and have the capacity to truly understand their feelings or situation requires a lot more effort.

Empathy requires shared experience and extensive communication. It requires that the leader become involved, at least to a certain level, in the situation and conditions others experience. It requires working together at some level as teammates. Empathy cannot be achieved or even approached by sitting in an office thinking about how to do things better. One of the most important statements in the *Wikipedia* definition previously mentioned is this one: *"People inside companies struggle to make intuitive decisions and often get fooled into believing they understand their business if they have quantitative research to rely upon."*

Traditionally, leadership groups try to take shortcuts to success by researching and studying outputs and trends, or by hiring "smart guys," consultants and outside problem solvers, to come in and study stuff to give them statistics and a quick, easy formula for success. Those in positions of authority often convince themselves they've made it to the top and they can now sit back and dictate success from the comfort of their office chair. From my perspective, they become lazy and somehow think that their past efforts, experience, or education have allowed them to achieve success and now they can use their accumulated knowledge to lead the organization to greater success from the top. They get "fooled" into thinking that they know what is actually going on today within their organization.

In a previous discussion, we talked about the old concept of "management by walking around." This is where it comes into play. In any organization, conditions and situations are in a constant state of change. Internally, there is change as employees come and go, processes are changed, equipment and technology advance, the environment shifts, and a myriad of other little adjustments occur daily. Nothing is the same today as it was yesterday, let alone back in the day when the person at the top of the organization was working down on the front lines. Effective leadership requires teamwork. Those led must believe that they are involved with an excellent organization that provides excellent products and services. They must believe that those who lead the organization truly care about the success of individual employees as well as the company.

Every person in the company must be focused daily on the mission and on performing at the level of excellence necessary to keep the organization on track to be its best. And, by the way, people intuitively recognize the difference between empathy and sympathy. They know if the leadership is truly involved, interested, and still relevant. They need frequent direct contact with those in leadership to be reassured that all is well and that the leaders here are in touch and truly interested in and concerned, showing empathy, with their situation. They need to be reminded of the mission and their role. They need to express their feelings to those who have influence on their situation.

Sympathy happens from a distance. Empathy happens up close, only through shared time and experience. True empathy on the part of those in leadership roles will result in an environment where all participants are more likely to be motivated to do their best because they know those leading the organization are interested and concerned enough to care and be involved. People need to know that everybody is on the team and everybody, top to bottom, is carrying their share of the load. This requires frequent direct contact and shared time between employees at all levels and those in leadership roles. Leaders need to get out and spend time with their subordinates. They need to walk around, ask questions, communicate their thoughts and plans, and solicit input from those doing the work out in the trenches. They need to express their appreciation to those doing the great work.

Market trends change daily too. Successful organizations must be in constant contact with those they serve, the customers. How much do you appreciate the restaurant manager who stops by your table, introduces himself or herself, and asks how well they did at preparing your meal? When the "company," represented by that manager, takes the time to find out how the customers feel and expresses true interest in satisfying each customer, it makes a huge difference. Only by continuously working with customers, talking to them, and developing empathy with them can the organization recognize how they feel and make the adjustments to stay on top and continue to be successful in the marketplace.

When customers believe that the organization cares about them and is providing goods and services that fulfill their needs, they will be loyal and bring in additional customers. Business will thrive. If customers believe that the company has lost touch and is no longer interested in their satisfaction or needs, they will go elsewhere. When customers are excited about the organization, it is contagious and they will spread the news.

Immediately, people notice and appreciate when leaders care about them, their success, and the success of the organization. They also know when there is no true empathy. They notice when there is an absence of contact from leadership. They recognize that things around them aren't right and that leadership doesn't know or really care to be involved. Employees will only rise to the level of the example set by those who lead. The benefit of setting the right example is that the people around the organization will also mirror that example in their contacts with each other and with their customers. It will become part of the organizational culture.

Sympathy feels nice, but people will choose to follow leaders who are truly empathetic to their situation.

21

SALESPEOPLE AND GOOD LEADERS, ETERNAL OPTIMISTS

"I have fished through fishless days that I remember happily without regret."
—Roderick Haig-Brown

WHEN I WAS EIGHT years old, I became involved in two activities that, unbeknownst to me, would influence the rest of my life. I joined Cub Scouts, and I began playing Little League baseball. Both of these activities required a certain amount of financial support from each participant, the majority of which, as is the same today, involved fundraising. The difference between the 1960s and today is that kids were allowed to roam the neighborhood unsupervised.

My first fundraiser for Cub Scouts, and for me for that matter, involved selling little heart-shaped boxes of valentine candy. I had a bunch of them to sell. My father, who was a single father, and who, to my dismay at the time, also believed I should learn to take a direct frontal approach to challenges, told me he expected me to sell all of this candy so I should go out and get to it. He gave me a couple of instructions about how to introduce myself and a little suggestion for a sales pitch then sent me alone out into the neighborhood.

For hours, I went door to door trying to get somebody to buy the rest of this candy. To this day, I also remember the nice lady who bought my last two boxes. I had been at it for hours, completely exhausted, frustrated, and a little depressed, and, as I knocked on the door, she opened it with a big smile. She listened patiently as I explained my mission and showed her my product. I'll never forget that big smile when she asked, "How many do you have left?" I told her, "Just two more, ma'am." She invited me into her living room and handed me some cash, saying, "Well then I'll take two."

As I walked home from her house, I had an overwhelming sense of accomplishment. I'm not sure I was ever so excited before or since. I wanted to run the whole way home just so I could get there and tell my father I'd finished the job and all the candy was sold. This process was repeated every year for Little League baseball with their community booster sticker sales and, in later years, with my newspaper route and trying to develop new customers. Later in life, I sold clothing on commission for a major retailer. Early on, I learned that success comes with persistence; it requires staying with your task until you succeed.

Lessons I learned during my various sales "careers" included the fact that rejection and failure are facts of life when you are a salesperson. Success only comes when you choose to ignore rejection and failure and continue to push forward. You must learn to treat every "no" as a step toward the final "yes," which is out there. I looked at it like this: There are always going to be a certain number of people who will tell you no whenever you are selling anything or presenting a new idea. If you can teach yourself to believe that each of those no's is a good thing because it's taking you closer to the actual buyer you haven't yet met, then you can push through them without becoming discouraged and giving up.

I've been selling some product or another now for over fifty years. I know for a fact that only true optimists can survive in sales. In fact, people who are truly optimists, almost to a fault, thrive in sales. All others get frustrated, give up, and move to other careers. You have to believe and be excited because you know the sale is out there. You have to believe that you "just haven't found it yet."

I like this definition of optimism.
Urban Dictionary: ***"optimism"***
Optimism is trust that things will get better no matter how bad they seem, looking for the best aspects of any situation, and the belief that good will inevitably triumph over evil.

An optimist looks at a rose and ignores the thorns. A pessimist focuses on the thorns, oblivious of the rose.

During my life, I've worked for and alongside some great leaders. I've been in various leadership roles as well, and I truly believe that undying optimism is a required trait for successful leadership. Every organization goes through difficult times. Sometimes, business is going through a downturn, events happen that negatively affect the market or community, personnel challenges come along that affect morale, and innumerable other events bring trouble to the entity. Just trying to build and grow by using a team of people, all of whom have their own personalities, is challenging to say the least.

The talented, effective leader must be able to visualize the goal and future success, possess the ability to focus beyond the present distractions, and push with anticipation toward fulfilling the mission of the organization. The talented effective, leader cannot become distracted and lose faith when encountering difficulties or obstacles to success. They must also communicate that optimism to those around them so that the whole team stays focused on their eventual good fortune and success.

I have several friends who spent careers as Navy SEALs. I've asked them what made the difference that allowed them to be successful in the program when the overwhelming majority of candidates fail during BUD/S and Hell Week. They each told me, "It's not who is the toughest, strongest, or biggest, but it's those people who can ignore their present extreme discomfort and unwaveringly focus on reaching the end successfully." They all said, "If you, for even the shortest time, become distracted by the cold, pain, and fatigue and lose your focus, you will fail. You have to know that in time this difficulty will end and you will achieve success. You must never stop believing."

Society is obsessed with finding and reporting bad news. It seems as if every media outlet makes its living by showing somebody failing at something. If they can't find bad news, they invent it. We as humans have a tendency to look for the bad news, to look for and obsess about that thing that will cause us to fail. We criticize each other and ourselves continuously and choose to believe that something bad is happening or about to happen. When good things happen to other people around us, we discredit that person for some other reason because it makes us feel better about ourselves. The world thrives on bad news.

This is the opposite of the outlook shared by all successful leaders and salespersons. Negativity cannot take control of the stage of our lives if we choose to spend our efforts leading others toward success. When negative thoughts take over, all motivation to continue stops. Failure appears as a likely outcome on the horizon, and we become distracted by trying to assess the damage that is about to occur or by trying to figure out who we should blame for this bad news. I like to compare it to water in the toilet. When the flush lever is pushed, the water spins round and round before it goes down the drain. Negativity in life means that our entire focus is on the problem right here at hand; we don't see the horizon or the future because we are focused on right here right now. We end up spinning around and around, getting nowhere, eventually going down in failure.

As a leader, we must be able to believe that, no matter how bad it looks right now, no matter how uncomfortable things are, there is a solution and we will work past this. We must be able to willfully make ourselves look past the present toward the eventual accomplishment of our mission. Successful results are out there, and the problems and difficulties we will for sure encounter on the way are just stepping stones to success. Each will be addressed, resolved, and put behind us so that we can move on to the next step and ultimately to the result we are seeking.

I'm not trying to say that great leaders cannot fail. What I'm saying is that the ability to see, focus, and move past the no's along the path is an unnatural skill for most of us. The ability to teach ourselves to expect positive outcomes and to work tirelessly, past one obstacle at a time, to reach them is a skill we must learn and develop. Our society does not teach us these things. We must teach ourselves and then we must mentor others so that they learn to do the same. The world is full of good things and good outcomes. Difficulties and challenges are merely the stepping stones that we must pass on the way to our success.

Never become distracted and derailed by temporary difficulties and obstacles.

22
EXCELLENCE INCLUDES HANDLING ALL THE DETAILS

"Fly-fishing for trout is like raising children, you never know what is going to happen next."
–Jimmy D. Moore

MOST CONVERSATIONS ABOUT EXCELLENCE involve the quality of a product or service that has been purchased. People talk about what a great item it was or wasn't, or what great service they received or didn't receive. They talk about how something did or did not meet their expectations. People talk about their favorite store, restaurant, dental office, teacher, or others because they always enjoy their visits there or they always deliver what they say they will. Most of us don't spend much time thinking about how excellence happens, but we certainly recognize it when we find it. We appreciate it and want more of it when we finally know where it is.

Something that excellent organizations know that others do not is that excellence is not just an item. It's a "feeling in the air," a "way of being" that people notice. Excellent places feel good to visit. When you walk in, you notice it. It's all around you, but you can't see it. What is that, and how does it happen?

In previous chapters, we've discussed how attitudes, focus, work effort, and a multitude of other aspects of group dynamics are contagious. Expectations and "the way we do things here" must be managed, modeled, and communicated from the very highest leadership position in the organization. With constant attention to this, they become the organizational personality, culture, or identity that employees and customers both notice.

Obviously, everybody wants quality products. We have all kinds of quality control checks, warranties, and testing processes to make sure our products meet the expectations. I can't tell you how many pairs of jeans I've purchased over the years that had a little piece of paper in the pocket telling me they were "inspected by no. 5." The important details go far beyond this though.

When I worked for Nordstrom in the 1970s and 1980s, members of the Nordstrom family visited all the stores regularly, unannounced. It wasn't uncommon for them to be around weekly or even more often than that. It was part of that whole "management by walking around" idea that worked so well. One visit that is still fresh in my memory happened while I was general manager of a store in Southern California. Jim Nordstrom, who was company president at the time, was visiting and invited me to take a walk out in the mall. We walked through all the major retail stores and just looked around. We discussed what the salespeople were doing, what the customers were doing, how things looked, and how things were set up. We went store by store, and I remember him saying, "I'm sure there's somebody somewhere who cares about this store, but that person is clearly not here."

After Jim Nordstrom made that comment, we walked back to my store. Notice that I said "my store"—that's how I viewed it. Right before we went in, he stopped me out in the mall and said, "Here's what I want you to do every time you walk into this store: I want you to take two steps in and stop and put yourself in the shoes of a first-time customer. Look around at everything and every person and ask yourself if it looks like the people here really care about their store. Is it clean and shiny? Are the salespeople smiling? Are they attentive and talking to the customers, or are they having a private conversation in the corner? Is the merchandise neat and orderly and hung up, or are there items on the floor? Do all the customers you see look satisfied, or are there people who look confused or unhappy? Are the signs and displays neat, clean, and orderly? Are there burned-out lights? Is there gum on the carpet? Is the ceiling clean? Does it look like they're proud of their store?"

I never forgot that lesson Jim Nordstrom shared with me that day, and I can say I passed that first test but it was a very humbling experience. *Does it feel good to enter here? Do you like to come here? Are the people here happy to see you? Do you feel important here?* His point was that it's not good enough to do this once. You have to do it every day, maybe multiple times every day, and every detail is important if you want people, both customers and employees, to feel the excellence when they come here. He also told me, "Our competitors come here and draw diagrams of how we have our sales floor set up. They think that's why we're doing well. Then we move the racks around every day, and they have to draw another diagram. They don't get it. They can't understand what makes us different. They'll never understand it."

The military and police and fire departments are masters of taking care of these details. They polish their equipment every day. Their clothing is clean, starched, and pressed. They train and practice continuously. They know that if you look good and you are trained and competent, you feel good. Professionalism involves knowing as well as looking like you have it together all the time. When I was in the police academy, our uniforms got inspected every day. We were asked questions about the previous day's study material. If there was lint or a wrinkle, or if a button was loose, or if we didn't know an answer, we did pushups, lots of pushups. The whole squad did pushups. The idea was the same. If you look good and you know your job and how to do it well, you feel good and people notice that. You gain credibility. They had to go through the process to help us understand that lesson. The interesting thing is that we have to work really hard to get there most of the time. We, as humans, don't just naturally think about the details and how important they are. We tend to just wander through life, getting by day by day.

Somebody, leadership, has to think about the details first and make them important. Then they have to go out, walk around, and communicate it. Then they have to look for excellence every day, expect it, demand it, teach people what it looks like, and equip their people to achieve it, train people to a high level of competence, and work on it every day. They have to teach every person to do the same, to view the details as important.

At Nordstrom, there was a time the leadership felt the stores weren't clean and shiny enough overall. They made it into a companywide contest and had surprise inspections multiple times throughout the year. They didn't just inspect the sales floor, they also checked storage areas, offices, stairwells, every part of the building. We talked about it every day. Each person in the organization became aware of it and did their part to achieve it. It made a huge difference. They did it every year for a while, and the winning stores were rewarded and recognized for their excellent attention to detail, companywide.

Soon, every store looked good. They were clean and shiny and people were proud of their store. That's my point here. The details—all of the details—are part of the process. Teaching people to see and be aware of, then to take care of the details, is one of the things that helps develop that atmosphere and feeling of pride and excellence. Those details are different organization by organization, but they are there everywhere and most of the time, at least some of them are overlooked.

It comes back to what Jim Nordstrom told me over thirty years ago. "I'm sure there's somebody somewhere who cares about this store, but that person is clearly not here." People notice excellence. They like and appreciate it and will want to return once they find it.

23

ARE DISTRACTIONS MOVING US AWAY FROM OUR MISSION?

"O sir, doubt not that angling is an art. Is it not an art to deceive a trout with an artificial fly?"
–Izaak Walton

ALL ORGANIZATIONS EXIST AND operate within a dynamic environment. There are many "moving parts." Every day, we interact with coworkers, customers, and the marketplace over and over. Some of us communicate internally with our own people. Some of us communicate with new or existing customers, read the comments and reviews, listen to news and rumors, watch our competitors' actions, and, in the end, try to interpret the information gathered during these interactions and apply that information to what we do and how we do it. We know that to succeed and grow in the world, each of us within our organizations must continually evaluate what we do, how we do it, and how well we are doing it. If we wish to be excellent, we must continually fine tune and make the adjustments necessary to grow and improve in an ever-changing world. How do we decide what we should change and what we should leave alone?

The world is a fast-moving, noisy place. Information bombards us. Accurately interpreting all of this information is the critical key to using it for our own benefit. If we just look at the current political environment, for example, we can see this in action. The parties, the media, the special interest groups, and the other players are continuously sending out information to influence public opinion. We know that some of this information is accurate, but we also hear talk of "fake news" that is mixed in. Many of the "facts" that are being reported contradict each other. There are reports of public surveys with contradicting information. How can that be if those reporting this information are truly acting within the boundaries of true and impartial practice? It becomes our responsibility to sort through all of the noise to identify and act on the information that will lead us to the most accurate conclusions. So it is within our own organizations too. We must pay careful attention to identify the critical information that will allow us to reach the very best conclusions, thereby generating the very best decisions.

Earlier, we discussed that it is good to welcome and even solicit feedback in the form of suggestions, recommendations, or even complaints. This helps us evaluate our current operations and identify opportunities to improve. The critical first step though is to continually focus on our mission. Many organizations allow themselves to become distracted and get away from what makes them great in the first place. It is easy, in our attempts to understand and respond to all this incoming information, to become distracted from our original path. Fires must be put out daily, crises must be addressed, conflicts must be resolved, and competitors' innovations must be addressed. Each of these requires our focus and attention until the next priority arises and we move on.

In time, it is likely that we, as an organization, will be tempted to become "lost in the details" and allow ourselves to make decisions and changes that cause us to be diverted away from our original path, which misdirects our trajectory away from the mission. How many major companies and organizations, when compared today to the original organization that was started by the earliest founders, bear very little resemblance whatsoever? Are they more excellent now or not? Have they lost focus, or have they stayed true to their mission?

Somewhere within this machine we call our organization, there must be somebody who continually goes back to that mission and watches to ensure that we are still on track. This must be in the forefront of communication with all of our employees and customers to keep the focus where it needs to be. We need to help people understand the necessity of interpreting all of this input they receive from the context of "how can we use it to be better at what we are trying to be."

As we look at this process, the obvious questions are, "How do we decide what to believe and how to respond to information we are receiving? How do we use and manage all of this input?" The critical components of this decision-making process are wisdom and restraint. Nobody likes "management by committee," but there is a benefit to bringing varied viewpoints, personalities, and opinions into the decision-making process. The balance now becomes one of having an organization that is "nimble" in the marketplace, able to adjust and move as necessary to stay in front, but not one that chases every whim and fancy that comes along, thereby becoming distracted and irrelevant over time.

We discussed that a key component of effective leadership is the willingness and ability to make timely decisions. Now, we add this additional component to that statement: Effective leadership requires the willingness and ability to make decisions that align with the organizational mission and that allow us to improve and grow without being distracted from our overall critical focus. Effective leadership embraces opportunities to improve and become more successful while, at the same time, safeguarding the overall values that make the organization what it is in the first place.

Ambition tempered with restraint and wisdom is the operative concept. This view must be communicated organization-wide so that every person understands the compelling need to improve and embrace growth but only within the framework of who we are and what we are striving to be. People need continual guidance to reinforce what that framework looks like. Each decision maker must understand the context of their guidelines and rules and be given the latitude to make the right decisions as needed. They need to understand how their decision fits within the organizational framework, and they must understand the big picture of how their piece of the process fits into the rest of the company. This allows them to make changes, adjustments, and decisions that are in the best interest of the whole organization and that contribute to the mission.

Once again, as in previous discussions, we understand that true leadership involves careful monitoring and communication of the overall mission of the organization. Change, growth, and improvement require continuous evaluation of ourselves and our environment and timely decision-making. To reiterate, a critical component is decision-making based upon wisdom, understanding, and restraint and the ability to identify and resist the temptation to respond to input that would distract us from the path we need to follow in our quest for excellence. Each person must know who we are, what makes us great, and how their role contributes to the overall mission. They then have the tools to make decisions and respond to changes in a way that supports the mission itself.

ACKNOWLEDGMENTS

I OWE A DEBT of gratitude to Nordstrom past officers, the late Jim Nordstrom, former president; Jack McMillan, former executive vice president; Bob Bender, former senior vice president; and Betsy Sanders, former regional vice president for Southern California, for believing in me at a young age and for their encouragement, teaching, mentoring, and, of course, scolding when I needed it. They allowed me to be a participant in something great that lit a lifetime fire in me to understand the dynamics of leadership and the path to excellence.

I also owe a debt of gratitude to former Snohomish County Sheriff Rick Bart for being there for me during a devastating personal tragedy. His true leadership and unwavering commitment to his people, and to me, were a strong example of what this book is about.

I have to thank my wife, Colleen, for her tireless encouragement, proofreading, and suggestions during the creation of this book. Without her support, I would never have been able to finish it.

www.ingramcontent.com/pod-product-compliance
Lightning Source LLC
Chambersburg PA
CBHW031858200326
41597CB00012B/470